creative

*Wedding florals*

you can make

Terry L. Rye

**BETTERWAY BOOKS**
Cincinnati, Ohio

Other fine Betterway Books are available from your local book-
store, art supply store or direct from the publisher.

10  09  08  07  06    12  11  10  9

Library of Congress Cataloging-in-Publication Data

Rye, Terry L.,
    Creative wedding florals you can make / by Terry L. Rye.
       p. cm.
    Includes index.
    ISBN-13: 978-1-55870-560-9 (pbk.)
    ISBN-10: 1-55870-560-0 (pbk.)
     1. Wedding decorations. 2. Flower arrangement. 3. Bridal
bouquets. I. Title.

SB449.5.W4 R94 2000
745.92'6—dc21

00-040185

Editor: Tricia Waddell
Designer: Stephanie Strang
Production coordinator: Emily Gross
Production artist: Lisa Holstein
Photographers: Christine Polomsky and Al Parrish

*I dedicate this book to*

*my spirited daughter, Sarah, and to my loving*

*family for their support and encouragement*

*throughout my life.*

**▸ about the author**

Terry Rye's passion for flowers has allowed her the best job in the world—creating innovative and beautiful floral designs. Since 1980 she has been the owner of The Mariemont Florist in Cincinnati, Ohio. The Mariemont Florist has been featured in the prestigious Cincinnati Flower Show and is listed in the distinguished international directory, Fine Flowers by Phone. As a self-taught floral designer, Terry loves to share the joy of floral arranging with others, especially for such a special occasion as a wedding. Terry resides in Cincinnati, Ohio, with her six-year-old daughter Sarah.

## *acknowledgments*

Many thanks to all the dedicated people in my business, The Mariemont Florist, for their support and loyalty during the completion of this book and for their contributions to the step-by-step design. I am truly blessed with a talented staff, wonderful friends and an incredibly supportive, loving family.

Many thanks to my editor, Tricia Waddell, for her encouragement and help in writing this, my first book. My life has been enriched by this experience. I will always be grateful to have been given this opportunity by Greg Albert at F&W Publications. Thanks also to Anne Bowling.

I also want to thank the Indian Hill Church in Cincinnati for the use of their sanctuary and beautiful entrance.

Most of all I want to thank my dear friend Laurie Tudor for always being there when I needed her on this project, and my wonderful six-year-old daughter, Sarah, who never let me lose sight of what is important in life . . . our loved ones.

# table of

**flowers for the bride**

**flowers for the bridal party**

*part one*

*part two*

24

62

**flowers for the wedding party**

**flowers for the ceremony & reception**

*part three*

76

*part four*

88

I have spent the past twenty years creating beautiful flower arrangments. Nothing makes me happier than to smell a rose, to watch a tulip unfold, to create a striking arrangement or to see a bride's face light up when she sees the beautiful bouquet I made especially for her. Time and again I've experienced the excitement of designing beautiful wedding flowers, and I've written this book to help you experience the same excitement and joy on one of your most memorable days—your wedding day!

Over the years I've encountered many brides on a limited budget who feel thay can't have the flowers they've always wanted because of the cost involved. What they often don't realize is that most of that cost can be attributed to the labor in making the arrangements, not the flowers, ribbons, tools and other supplies. This book will show you how easily you can create beautiful arrangements yourself, which not only allows you to realize your vision of the perfect wedding but will also add a unique and personal touch to your wedding and help you save a few dollars.

Whether you are the bride-to-be, a member of the wedding party, a friend of the happy couple or an aspiring floral designer, this book will guide you in creating wedding flowers easily with striking results. You will learn how to plan and coordinate your wedding flowers, whether you want to make all the arrangements yourself or work in tandem with a professional florist to achieve exactly the look that expresses your personality. The following pages show over twenty creative floral arrangements that you can re-create step-by-step or use as inspiration. Not only will I walk you through each project, I will also share lots of tips that will help you think and work like an experienced florist. So start making your vision of the perfect wedding a reality. The imagination, enthusiasm and creativity you pour into your floral arrangements will result in priceless memories for yourself and your guests. Enjoy!

TERRY L. RYE

The key to successful wedding flowers is planning. Whether you design your own floral arrangements, have your florist create them or work in tandem with your florist, there are some issues you need to consider. Here are the main items you'll need to address—no matter who does your flowers.

*Colors* Your wedding colors (including your wedding dress, bridesmaids' dresses, tuxes, etc.) should be one of the first things you determine *before* you start planning your wedding flowers. Your color theme and wedding style will determine the atmosphere at both the ceremony and the reception. Choose flowers that complement and enhance your chosen themes to create a unified look.

Look through books and magazines to see what colors best create the look you want. Experiment with different combinations to get an idea of what colors you want to emphasize and which ones you want to be more subtle.

When selecting flowers, consider how they will look when photographed. If, for instance, your bridesmaids have light lavender dresses and you make bouquets full of lavender flowers, the flowers in the bouquet may fade into the dress because there isn't enough contrast. Remember, you want your flowers to look as spectacular in your wedding photos as they looked on your wedding day.

# planning your wedding flowers

Planning a wedding is an exciting and creative opportunity to design the look and feel of the event the way you've always envisioned it, especially with flowers! Here are some guidelines for planning the wedding flowers of your dreams.

8

*Personal style* To determine your personal vision and style, ask yourself some questions. Are you gregarious? Subdued? Serious? Lighthearted? What do you definitely *not* like? Be honest about who you are and what you want. Are you the spontaneous type who might gather loose garden flowers in your hand to walk down the aisle? Or are you elegant, preferring a sophisticated floral style that requires a few dramatic flowers? Maybe you want to keep it simple—carrying just one long, dramatic calla lily down the aisle. Think about who you are, what you like, and what your flower arrangements will express about you and your wedding day. That's how you'll discover and define your personal wedding style.

*Mood and atmosphere* Even before the ceremony starts, your floral presentation will establish the mood of your wedding. To figure out what flower combinations will create the particular mood you're looking for, look at photographs of various arrangements and ask yourself how each picture makes you feel. Then think about how you want to feel on your wedding day and you'll soon know what flowers will create the mood you want.

Remember, though, that you're going for more than just a style or color; you're looking for specific flowers that create your desired mood. Red roses convey a different mood than red carnations, for example.

When considering mood and atmosphere, don't forget to consider how you want your guests to feel at your wedding. Do you want them to feel warm? Relaxed? Formal? Impressed? Make mental notes of weddings you've been to and how you felt. What was it about the decorations that caught your attention? How did they make you feel? This will help you design wedding flowers that help your guests get in the right mood at your wedding.

Your bridal bouquet is probably the first arrangement of flowers you begin designing in your mind. There are many shapes and styles of bouquets to choose from. Here's a run-down on the different types of bouquets you can carry down the aisle.

Cascade · A traditional, full-flowing bouquet with long-stemmed flowers extended out to create a waterfall effect.

Nosegay · A round bouquet (16" to 18" [41cm to 46cm] in diameter) with densely packed flowers.

Biedermeier · A round bouquet tightly composed of expanding rings of individual colors or flowers.

Crescent · An arched bouquet featuring several full flowers with trailing flowered stems on both sides to form a crescent shape.

Hand-Tied · A natural bouquet of flowers tied together with ribbons. Often the stems are left showing.

Pomander · A flower-covered ball suspended from a loop of ribbon.

*Time of day* The time of day when your wedding is scheduled can affect the design of your wedding flowers. If your wedding takes place in the morning or afternoon, you might want to rule out floral arrangements with candles, especially if the wedding is outside or in a hall with many windows. Many brides want to have candles—even in the middle of the day—but if there's a lot of light coming into the room, the candles won't create the atmosphere you want. Also, if you are doing your own flowers, you may want to schedule your wedding later in the day to give yourself plenty of time for any last-minute flowers and setup.

*Outdoor Weddings* The most important issue when planning flowers for an outdoor wedding is temperature. Some flowers do not hold up well under some weather conditions. If it's too hot or too cold, many flowers will wilt quickly after they're cut. For instance, daisies, roses, lilies, alstroemeria, carnations and mums hold up well in the heat. Other flowers, such as gardenias, tulips, stephanotis and irises, wilt in high temperatures. If you choose a flower prone to wilting in the summer heat, use it sparingly so if it wilts it will be less noticeable. Check with a florist to choose the best flowers for an outdoor celebration. Another option is to use silk flowers instead of fresh ones. In all of the projects in this book, silk flowers can be substituted for fresh and vice versa.

When setting up flowers for an outdoor wedding, make sure your table arrangements are properly anchored, especially if you want height in your

arrangements. (Your florist can suggest ways to do this depending on the arrangement.) Bud vases, which are typically very light, can easily blow over on a reception table. An outdoor wedding on a pretty day certainly is beautiful, but keep in mind that a strong breeze can ruin a good floral arrangement.

Finally, don't forget about bees. Some flowers, such as freesia, gardenias, roses and lilies, have strong fragrances that draw bees, especially in warm weather. Also, any flowers with visible stamens may draw bees, so be sure to carefully remove the stamens to avoid attracting insects.

*Season* The most important reasons to choose flowers that are in season at the time of your wedding are availability and cost. It will be easier to find the flowers you want if they are in season. Although you can have flowers shipped in from other regions, out-of-season flowers can be costly. Check the Flower & Foliage Glossary on page 22 to find out the seasonal availability of popular wedding

flowers. You can also check with your florist to see when your favorite flowers are in season, or you can use silk flowers if the flowers you want won't be in season on your wedding day.

*Fragrance* The smell of flowers permeating the air at your wedding is a nice touch, but be careful not to overdo it. Fragrant flowers en masse can be overpowering. You can consult with a florist to find out which flowers have soft fragrances that aren't too potent. Flowers that tend to have overpowering fragrances are gardenias, Stargazer lilies and Casa Blanca lilies. These flowers all have a wonderful scent and are lovely when used sparingly, but if they're in a closed, warm room the scent can be overwhelming.

*Containers* Finding your own containers for your wedding flowers can be so much fun and a great way to get your fiancé involved in the wedding plans. Keep in mind that you don't necessarily have to use the same container on every table. Many couples have a wonderful time scouring garage sales and flea markets for a mix and match of containers that go well together. Even if you want a florist to create some of the table arrangements, she can use your hand-picked containers. Not only is this a great way to personalize your wedding and reception, it's a good, cost-saving way to blend the florist's creativity with your own. Just give yourself plenty of time to find containers: it can be hard to find thirty or more vases (even ones that match) at the last minute.

*Cost* Today the budget-minded bride can easily have the wedding she wants. One simple but not so obvious way to save money is to find a florist who will get to know you and care for your needs—you want more than just an order-taker. You should be open about your budget—don't be embarrassed. The more the florist knows about you and what you can afford, the better off you'll be. You may, for instance, want lily of the valley but have no idea that it will cost five times as much in December than in May. A florist with a good idea of your budget will tell you this and help you make a more suitable selection.

There are many other ways to manage costs. If you make some or all of the ceremony and reception flowers yourself, you'll really lower your expenses. In the summer you could use natural foliage and flowers out of your garden.

## arranging your own wedding flowers

Many brides want to create their own floral arrangements because they want to save money, personalize their wedding or just have fun with flower arranging. But before you dive in headfirst and tell the world you're doing everything on your own, take a minute to ask yourself these important questions to ensure that creating your own wedding florals is an enjoyable and successful experience.

· Which flowers would be the least stressful for me to do myself, from making the arrangements to delivering them?

· Can I honestly have the flowers ready for the wedding and reception in time?

· If I do my own reception flowers, will I have enough time before the wedding to set them up at the reception site, or should I get someone else to do it?

· How easily can I transport the flowers to the reception? Will I need a car, van or truck?

· Can I box the flowers myself for easy and safe transport?

· Do I have a cool place to store the flowers and finished arrangements before the wedding?

· Do I have enough family and friends to help me with making, transporting and setting up the flowers?

While there is a lot to think about, if you address these questions early, you can do your own flowers and have a blast. Just try to anticipate any last-minute problems and call your florist for assistance and guidance.

You could also limit your wedding party so you have fewer bouquets and boutonnieres to buy. Also, remember that flowers for a holiday wedding will be more expensive because flowers are in high demand at these times of year. If you are having a holiday wedding, you may want to do many of the arrangements yourself to cut down on costs. Creativity is the best way to save on costs so you can have the wedding you want on a reasonable budget.

*Silk and Dried Flowers* While silk flowers have always been a less popular option for wedding flowers, the high quality of today's silk flowers makes them a wonderful alternative to fresh flowers. And the best aspect of silk flowers is that they make wonderful keepsake gifts for the bridal party. Another way to use silk flowers is to add in a few fresh flowers to accent a silk bouquet or arrangement on the day of your wedding.

Bridal party bouquets, corsages, boutonnieres, pew decorations and centerpieces are the most common places where silk flowers are used (from a distance, guests will never know the difference). Dried flowers are also playing a more important role these days in autumn weddings and they make great keepsake gifts.

## working with a florist

When you are planning your wedding flowers, one way to make arranging your own flowers more manageable is to divide them up with your florist. For example, maybe you want to do your own reception table flowers, but you would rather have your florist make the bridal party

bouquets. This is a great way to save money and also have the guidance of a professional in designing your flowers. The key to collaborating with a florist is communication. So be sure to thoroughly interview potential florists to make sure you can work together well.

*Choosing a Florist* Ideally, you should contact a florist three to six months before your wedding date. By the time you meet with a florist you should have already decided the following aspects of your wedding: the time, the date, the ceremony and reception sites, the bridal gown and attendants' dresses, the color and style of the groomsmen's tuxes, the size of the wedding party, the number of guests, your overall color theme and your flower budget.

The first step in selecting a florist is finding somebody who is open to your participation. Your florist should be a good listener and easy to work with. The florist should ask you about your ideas and opinions, not just tell you what to do. It's your responsibility to let the florist know if you want to do decorations in conjunction with her. If she indicates that she wants to do it all by herself, you immediately know she's not the florist for you.

You also want a florist who asks the right questions. She should ask questions such as: What part are you interested in being involved in and how can I help you? How do you want me to help you make this a special, relaxed day? It's also important to ask how much the florist will be willing to help you with your projects if you run into problems.

You also want to make sure your florist won't have several other weddings on the same day as yours. It's your wedding day and you need and deserve individual attention, especially at the last minute. Do your best to ensure the florist has the available staff to handle your setup. If you really like a potential florist but find she has other weddings coinciding with yours, perhaps you could figure out a way to increase your involvement. Offering to do the setup yourself is one way to help out and this will also cut down on your florist costs.

A good florist will also be willing to provide you with cost-cutting information. She can let you know which areas of wedding floral arranging are the most labor-intensive and how you could lower these costs. Corsages and wedding bouquets, for example, are quite labor intensive, as is a lot of the setup. Put these costs together and the bill can get pretty high—and that doesn't count the cost of the flowers! Your florist should itemize all the prices for you and discuss alternative, cost-saving options.

*Delineating Responsibilities* Make sure that, before you meet with your florist to discuss collaborating, you have an idea of what flowers you want to handle yourself. Let her know that you want her professional expertise in suggesting ideas, choosing flowers, ordering supplies and coordinating all the flowers.

After you meet with your florist it's important that you both have a very clear sense of what you're each responsible for. You don't want to get into one of those "Well I thought *you* were going to do that" discussions on your wedding day. So be extremely clear about who's responsible for what. Write down every detail and make sure both you and your florist have updated copies of this document at all times.

# wedding flower plan

*You have decided which flowers you want to do yourself, chosen a florist to work with, and selected your wedding gown, bridal party, wedding style and color themes. Now it's time to lay out your floral plan. Use this form as a checklist for your floral needs and budget. Get all your thoughts down on paper and use this as a guide when ordering flowers and supplies and while working with your florist to ensure you have everything covered, from meeting your budget needs to timely flower delivery.*

## The Bride

| | |
|---|---|
| Color and style of dress | |
| Style of bouquet | |
| Flowers | $ |
| Bouquet to throw | $ |
| Hairpiece | $ |

## The Bridal Party

| | | |
|---|---|---|
| Number of honor attendants | Price of each bouquet $ | $ |
| Color and style of dresses | | |
| Style of bouquets | | |
| Flowers | | |
| Hairpiece | Price of each hairpiece $ | $ |
| Number of bridesmaids | Price of each bouquet $ | $ |
| Color and style of dresses | | |
| Style of bouquets | | |
| Flowers | | |
| Hairpiece | Price of each hairpiece $ | $ |
| Number of junior bridesmaids | Price of each bouquet $ | $ |
| Color and style of dresses | | |
| Style of bouquets | | |
| Flowers | | |
| Hairpiece | Price of each hairpiece $ | $ |
| Number of flower girls | Price of each bouquet $ | $ |
| Color and style of dresses | | |
| Style of bouquets | | |
| Flowers | | |

| | | |
|---|---|---|
| Hairpiece | Price of each hairpiece $ | $ |
| Number of Ringbearers | | |
| Boutonnieres | Price of each boutonniere $ | $ |
| Flower accessories | Price of each accessory $ | $ |

## Boutonnieres

| | | |
|---|---|---|
| Number | Price of each boutonniere $ | |
| Groom | Best Man | Groomsmen |
| Ushers | Fathers | Grandfathers |
| Minister | Others | $ |

## Corsages

| | | |
|---|---|---|
| Bride's mother: dress color | Flowers | $ |
| Groom's mother: dress color | Flowers | $ |
| Grandmothers: | | $ |
| Organist/Pianist | | $ |
| Vocalist | | $ |
| Hostesses: number | Price of each corsage $ | $ |
| Flowers | | |
| Honored guests and others | | $ |
| | | $ |

## Church Decorations

| | | |
|---|---|---|
| Delivery Time | | |
| Altar flowers | | $ |
| Other flower arrangements | | $ |
| Aisle and pew decorations: number | Price of each $ | $ |
| Candelabra | | $ |
| Other | | $ |

## Reception

| | | |
|---|---|---|
| Place | | Delivery Time |
| Bridal table | | $ |
| Guest tables:number | Price of each centerpiece $ | $ |
| Centerpiece flowers | | |
| Other flowers/accents | | $ |
| Cake table | | $ |
| Cake flowers | | $ |
| Buffet table arrangements: number | Price of each arrangement $ | $ |
| Arrangement flowers | | $ |
| Guest book table | | $ |
| Gift table | | $ |
| Other | | $ |

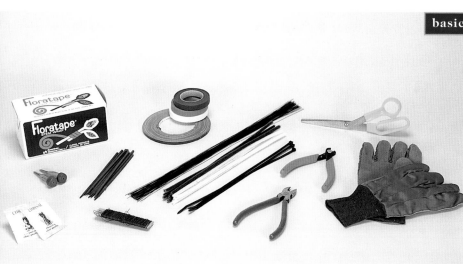

# basic tools

## &

## supplies

Before you get started on the step-by-step arrangements on the following pages, it's a good idea to familiarize yourself with the basic tools and floral supplies you will need to successfully create your wedding flowers.

**Cable Ties** · Cable ties are available at your local hardware store and can be found in many lengths. They are ideal for securing hand-tied bouquets.

**Chenille Stems** · Chenille stems are similar to pipe cleaners and are used in securing bows and for strengthening stems. They consist of bendable, twisted, heavy wire and a flocked material that allows water to flow through.

**Floral Preservatives** · Floral preservatives, such as Chrysal Clear, contain vital plant nutrients to help your flowers stay fresher, longer. These can be obtained from any florist.

**Floral Picks** · Wooden floral picks come in several sizes and are useful in securing bows in bouquets and extending stem lengths. All the projects throughout this book use 4" (11cm) floral picks from J.W. Cowee.

**Floral Wire** · This wire comes in different weights, or gauges. For the arrangements in this book you will need 24-gauge wire. Floral wire is used to strengthen stems and bind flowers together.

**Floral Tape** · Used to wrap floral stems and secure flowers together, floral tape is available in white and dark and light green.

**Garden Gloves** · Gloves are ideal for stripping thorns and unwanted leaves from stems safely.

**Floral Foam Tape** · Floral foam tape comes in white or green and is available in various widths. It is also used to wrap stems and secure arrangments.

**Paddle Wire** · This wire comes wrapped around a paddle for ease in holding with one hand to secure and wrap a group of stems, as in a garland. Paddle wire can be found at your local florist or craft store.

**Water Tubes** · These tubes are filled with water and used to add fresh flowers to silk or dried bouquets as well as to potted plants. Water tubes are available in various lengths based on the size of your project and where they will be placed in the arrangement.

**Wire Cutters** · You need easy-to-handle wire cutters to cut thin-stemmed silk flower stems or dried material. For heavier stems, a stronger pair may be necessary.

**Floral Foam** · There are dry and wet foams. Dry foam is for silk and dried flower projects and is more dense and firm than wet foam. Wet foam absorbs liquid and holds its shape for arranging fresh flowers while keeping stems moist. Wet foam should be soaked very slowly. Be sure to float it on top of the water and let it absorb on its own. Do not push it into the water. Place the holes of the foam face down into the water for total absorption. Oasis is a common brand name for floral foam.

**Round Igloo Cages** · These small, round cages are easy to design with. They come in different sizes and are great for cake-top decorations and centerpieces that do not require containers.

**Square Cage** · This square plastic cage holds a whole brick of floral foam and provides a grid framework for arranging flowers.

**Bouquet Holders** · Bouquet holders are available in many shapes and styles and can contain dry or wet foam. The handles also come in varied styles.

**Foam Ring** · Foam rings come in many diameters and have a plastic backing for support. They can be used to make everything from door wreaths to candle rings.

**Design Master Sealers and Floral Paints** · These sprays are great for enhancing fresh flower colors and terrific for sealing dried material to maintain color and prevent breakage.

**Elmer's Glue** · Elmer's is a universal glue that can be used as a substitute for floral adhesives to secure silk and fresh flowers.

**Floor Wax** · Instead of cleaning and shining foliage with leaf shine, you can dip leaves in floor wax. Also, ivy is very popular for weddings, but can prematurely wilt. Dipping ivy in floor wax can help keep it fresh and attractive.

**Flora Lock** · Flora Lock by Lomey is a concentrated spray for securing stems in wet foam so they don't slip out.

**Floral Scents** · Available in various floral fragrances, these sprays are a wonderful way to enhance the fragrance of a wedding bouquet.

**Hairspray** · Aerosol hair spray can be used as a dried flower sealer.

**Floral Adhesive** · Floral adhesive is a dependable glue for wet or dry surfaces. It does not require heating and dries clear. For best results, add it to a surface and let it sit until it is tacky before adhering it.

**Leaf Shine** · Leaf shine is essential for cleaning foliage and giving it a waxy, crisp look. It also helps keep greenery from drying out too quickly.

17

BASIC TOOLS & SUPPLIES

## Wiring Flowers

Often it is necessary to wire flower stems to make them easier to work with. Here's an easy way to prepare your flowers.

**1** Insert a 6" (16cm) floral wire into the base of the flower head and pull it through. Leave equal lengths of wire on both sides of the flower base.

**2** Pull the ends of the wire down and in line with the stem to begin the wrapping process.

**3** Begin the wrapping process using floral tape. Floral tape does not have a right or wrong side. It becomes tacky and adheres to itself as it is stretched. Hold the flower with one hand and the tape in the other. Begin by stretching and pulling the tape downward. Twist the stem with the thumb and forefinger of one hand. As you twist, the tape should cover the stem snugly, overlapping on its way down the stem.

**4** Wrap the ends of the wire and press the tape snugly up and around to cover any exposed wire.

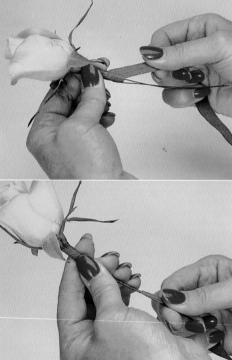

# basic
# techniques

This section details some of the basic techniques of flower arranging that you will use throughout this book.

18

## Strengthening Stems

Hollow-stemmed flowers such as gerbera daisies, daffodils and tulips will flop over quickly if the stems are not strengthened. Here's a florist's trick for keeping these flowers standing tall.

Insert the end of a chenille stem or floral pick into the base of the stem. Try to keep the stem straight with one hand and slowly insert with the other. You will not always be able to insert the chenille stem or floral pick all the way up the stem. Insert only until you feel resistance. Going up the stem even two-thirds of the way will help strengthen the stem and keep it from prematurely wilting.

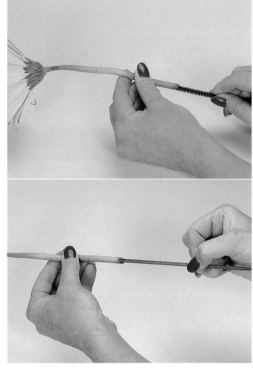

*top to bottom:* CHENILLE STEM, FLORAL PICK

## Stripping Thorns and Leaves

Many types of flowers and foliage are very thorny, including roses, sprengeri and plumosa. Here's how to clean stems safely and quickly.

To remove thorns and clean stems safely, it is helpful to wear garden gloves. Hold the foliage or rose with one hand. With the other hand, grab the stem where you want to begin stripping the foliage and thorns and pull downward on the stem tightly.

*top to bottom:* REMOVING PLUMOSA THORNS, REMOVING ROSE THORNS

## Cutting Stems

Where you cut a stem can affect its ability to draw water up to the flower head. Here's the best way to cut stems to prevent wilting.

Cut flower stems at a slant while they are in water for best results. For flowers such as roses and carnations, cut the stem above or below the noticeable nodules along the stems. This will allow water to easily reach the flower head. It will also help a flower open fully.

## Preserving Flowers

Fragile white flowers such as gardenias, stephanotis, freesia and lilac can easily bruise, brown or prematurely wilt, especially in high temperatures. Here's a helpful hint for keeping these delicate flowers looking good in your wedding bouquets and arrangements without sacrificing their wonderful scents.

To keep fragile white flowers looking white and fresh, hold the stem and dip the flower head in a glue mixture of approximately one tablespoon of Elmer's glue and one cup of water. Let it dry for five minutes.

PRESERVING A GARDENIA

## Adding Shine to Leaves

Want to make the foliage in your arrangements stand out? Using floral products such as leaf shine can keep your foliage from looking dull and lifeless.

Freely spray leaf shine on foliage and stems from a distance of approximately 10" (26cm). Let dry for five minutes before using in an arrangement or apply to foliage in an arrangement before the flowers are added.

## Opening Silk Flowers

Generally, new silk flowers need to be opened and prepared before you begin an arrangement. Here's an easy way to bring your silk flowers to life.

**1** Most silk flower stems are folded up like this lily stem when you first buy them.

**2** Begin unfolding the flower from the bottom. Start with the leaves and work your way up the stem.

**3** Now open the flowers and arrange the petals as naturally as you can.

**4** Your silk flower takes on a fresh look when unfolded and molded by your hands.

# bowmaking 101

Bows are often the finishing touch on wedding bouquets, corsages, decorations and arrangements. Here's a fool-proof course in making beautiful bows to complete your wedding flowers.

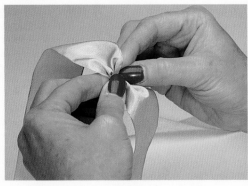

**1** Keeping the ribbon on the bolt, begin by pinching the ribbon between your fingers approximately 12" (31cm) from the end of the ribbon. That end piece of ribbon will become the first streamer of the bow. If 12" (31cm) is not long enough, pinch further up the ribbon and make the streamer as long as you desire.

**2** Begin by making the center loop of the bow. Twist the ribbon with your fingers and form a small hoop. Pinch the ribbon together in the center with your beginning streamer.

**3** Continuing to hold the bow in the center, twist the leading part of your ribbon and make a larger loop that will become the start of your actual bow. The size of the loop will determine the width of your bow. As you complete the loop bring the ribbon back to the center of the bow.

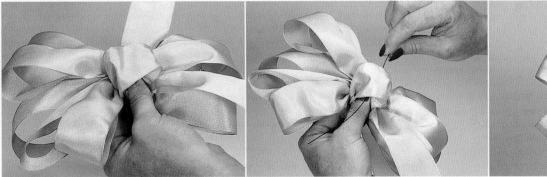

**4** Always twist the ribbon in the center before beginning a new loop. Now repeat making loops continuously from side to side until your bow is as full as desired. Four to five loops on a side is a common size. Continue holding the bow pinched with your fingers around the center and cut your ribbon from the bolt, leaving a second streamer approximately the same length as your starting streamer.

**5** Secure your bow by threading a floral wire through it. Pull the wire evenly through the bow, bring the wire ends to the back of the bow and twist tightly around the center of the bow.

**6** Now you have a finished bow. If you want to add more streamers, cut a piece of ribbon about double the length of the existing streamers. Don't worry about being exact—streamers look better when they are varying lengths. Pinch the center of the additional ribbon streamer and secure it with the wire holding the bow together. Adjust the loops attractively on both sides and trim the ends of the streamers with a diagonal or V-cut.

Here's your guide to the most popular wedding flowers. Use this glossary to find out when your favorite flowers are in season and the range of available colors.

**Acacia** Acacia is a soft, yellow flower with wonderful foliage for a distinctive look whether it is fall or spring time. It is best from October through March.

**Alstroemeria** Alstroemeria is a trumpet-shaped flower with an array of flower clusters at the top of the stem. It is a favorite and affordable wedding flower available in a variety of colors. This abundant flower stem is available year-round.

**Baby's Breath (Gypsophila)** This ball-shaped flower is a wonderful airy accent to all wedding bouquets. It is available year-round in white and shades of pink.

**Button Mums** A favorite for fall weddings, this flower is very hardy. Mums can withstand hot temperatures and be without water for hours. They are available year-round.

**Carnation** Carnations are round, large headed flower that can tolerate hot temperatures for summer weddings. With an endless color selection, carnations are popular flowers available year-round at an affordable price.

**Caspia (Limonium)** Caspia is a delicate, light, accent flower that is available year-round. With a trace of blue, caspia is great for a garden look bouquet. It is easy to arrange with and dries well too.

**Coffee** This crisp, dark green foliage is becoming a new favorite in wedding arrangements. The waxy leaves are abundant on a soft woody stem.

**Corkscrew Willow** Corkscrew or curly willow is a favorite for dramatic wedding designs. These branches are available year-round and in various lengths. The tips of the branches are an ideal accent in bouquets.

**Daisy Mums** Daisy mums are favorites for fall as well as spring weddings. This crisp looking flower is available year-round and is inexpensive.

**Delphinium** Delphinium is a tall and heavy flower-clustered stem that comes in white and shades of lavender, purple and pink. Available year-round, this elegant flower is popular in hand-tied bouquets.

**Eucalyptus** Eucalyptus dries attractively, is easy to arrange and is popular in long trailing bouquets. The leaves have a bluish green to silvery grey cast and are available year-round.

**Eucalyptus, Seeded Feather** This type of eucalyptus is lighter and airier than the traditional variety and is becoming increasingly popular among brides. This foliage is also a favorite for drying.

**Freesia** Freesia is among the most fragrant flowers. This beautiful, elegant, bell-shaped flower is available year-round and is a delicate addition to bridal bouquets.

**Gardenia** This abundantly fragrant flower is a classic wedding flower. Off-white in appearance, it can be used during any season. Gardenias have a large open blossom and are an elegant choice for any bouquet.

**Gerbera Daisy** Gerbera daisies are bright, colorful flowers available in a rainbow of colors. This round, vibrant daisy is available year-round in both large and miniature varieties.

**Heather** This long-stemmed flowering branch is a dramatic addition to long, trailing bouquets. Heather is available from November to April in white, lavender and pink.

**Hydrangea** The full and abundant hydrangea is available from March through September. This elegant flower is bright, delicate and can be easily dried. It is available in lavender, white and green.

**Ivy** Ivy is available with medium to dark green leaves and also with variegated leaves for unique designs. This foliage is a favorite in wedding design and is suited equally for elegant ceremonies and garden weddings.

**Leatherleaf Fern** Leatherleaf is the most common and affordable foliage. It is dark green in color and can be found year-round.

**Lemonleaf (Salal)** A popular foliage option, lemonleaf has broad, dark green leaves. It is available year-round.

**Lily, Asiatic** This star-shaped lily is a favorite in wedding design and enhances any bouquet with color and style. Asiatic lilies come in a wide array of colors and can be found year-round. They do not have a fragrance.

**Lily, Casa Blanca** Casa Blanca lilies are elegant, classic, white blooms perfectly suited for weddings. Casa Blancas are fragrant flowers and are available year-round.

**Lily, Stargazer** This regal and extremely fragrant flower is a favorite for its large bloom and brilliant colors of white and pink with red accents. It is available year-round.

**Orchid, Dendrobium** Dendrobium orchids are butterfly shaped orchids on a long, flowing stem. This flower is wonderful for cascading bouquets and can be found year-round.

**Plumosa** This dark green foliage adds a delicate, lacy look to any arrangement. It is very affordable and available year-round.

**Queen Anne's Lace** This round white flower is available year-round. It is a romantic filler flower for wedding bouquets, adding a Victorian touch to any design.

**Rose** The rose is a classic choice among brides. Its soft and fragrant bloom makes it an elegant choice in any bridal bouquet. Color selection is almost endless. While roses are available year-round, they are the most affordable during the summer months.

**Rose, Sweetheart** The sweetheart rose is a petite version of the classic rose and a very popular choice among brides for corsages and accents in bridal bouquets. Sweetheart roses are available year-round but are most affordable during the summer months.

**Ruscus, Italian** Italian ruscus has small, green, waxy leaves on multi-branching stems. Available year-round, it is an elegant accent foliage in any arrangement.

**Sprengeri (Asparagus Fern)** Sprengeri is an elegant, lacy accent foliage for all wedding designs. It is dark green and available year-round. Sprengeri can be used as filler foliage and is also great in long trailing bouquets.

**Statice** This very vivid flower is popular as filler. Statice can be used in fresh or dried bouquets and is available in purple and white. It is grown year-round.

**Stephanotis** This traditional wedding flower is a favorite in bridal bouquets. Stephanotis blossoms are white, fragrant and star-shaped. It is available year-round.

**Strawberry Bush (Leptospermum)** The dramatic, heavy, woodsy look of this flower makes it a favorite addition to winter bridal bouquets. Strawberry bush is a durable flower that appears in white and shades of pink and red. It is available from September through June.

**Tulips** The tulip gives a bright, fresh, springtime feeling to any wedding. It is not recommended during the summer months or for hot days because it will wilt. Color selection is endless and it is available October through May.

**Waxflower** Waxflower clusters are a popular alternative to baby's breath for creating a fresh new look in bridal bouquets. Their delicate and vivid waxy petals are shaped like small daisies in true white, pink or lavender. January through May are the best months for availability.

**Yarrow** This striking, dried-looking flower is available fresh and can be dried easily. It is generally available in shades of yellow and is a great choice for fall weddings.

one

Your bridal bouquet is the one collection of flowers that will most express the beauty and joy you are feeling on your wedding day. The flowers in your bouquet will make the most lasting impression on your guests as you walk down the aisle, and the look and scent of these flowers will forever remind you and your groom of your fondest wedding memories. So take some time to think about what you want your bouquet to express about you on your special day. After all, your bouquet is the signature accessory you will carry down the aisle when all eyes are on you, and it will also appear in all the photos.

How do you get those flowers to say something about you? The style of dress you are wearing and the overall tone of the wedding will help you determine the type of bouquet and selection of flowers you should carry. (See the sidebar on page 9 for a complete list of the various types of bouquets.) Be sure to pick a bouquet style that complements your dress and personality. The choices are endless based on your personal taste and the style of your wedding, so take the time to look at examples of bouquets from books and magazines to gather ideas.

Once you decide on the type of bouquet you want, it's time to choose the perfect flowers. Talk to a florist to find out which flowers are in season. Select flowers that reflect your personal vision and coordinate with your ceremony and reception flowers. You can also coordinate your bouquet with floral hair accessories to complete your look. Ultimately you want to weave all of your wedding flowers together, creating a singular, harmonious statement about you and your wedding.

With the above in mind, it's easy to see why brides invest a lot of time creating their personal flowers. More than any other flowers in your wedding, your bouquet is the arrangement that will be most associated with you. So design a bouquet you truly love, one that expresses all the beauty, romance and joy you are feeling on this most extraordinary day.

*flowers*
for the
*bride*

# *rose*

## cascade bouquet

*As the eternal symbol of love and romance, roses have long been a popular choice for brides. This classic off-white rose cascade bouquet is perfect for the bride who revels in romantic elegance.*

**◆ materials**

20–30 roses

2–3 stems baby's breath

6–8 stems leatherleaf

6–8 stems sprengeri fern

large floral foam bouquet holder

statice (optional)

leaf shine

Flora Lock

### 1 Outline With Leatherleaf

Saturate the floral foam holder and outline the outside of the bouquet with tips of leatherleaf. Add a longer stem of leatherleaf at the base to form the cascade shape. Strip the lower leaves off each stem and push the stems into the foam.

### 4 Spray With Leaf Shine

Spray with leaf shine until the entire bouquet is lightly covered and glossy.

### 2 Stagger Leaves

With smaller tips of leatherleaf, continue outlining the holder in layers, staggering the leaves for even coverage.

### 3 Add Sprengeri Fern

Trim off small pieces of fern. Strip the ends of the stems by wrapping a towel around the stems and pulling firmly down the stem. The towel will protect your hands from thorns. Fill in the foam holder with fern stems, using a longer stem at the base to shape the cascade.

### 5 Insert Roses

Remove the thorns from the rose stems. Pull off the leaf clusters except those up close to the rose bud. To gauge the length of the rose stem, hold a rose over the holder and cut the stem to the desired length. Add 1" (3cm) to allow for the part of the stem that will be pushed into the holder. Make sure the roses can be seen above the greenery.

### 6 Add Stem Adhesive

Spray stem adhesive on rose stems as they are inserted into the bouquet holder to hold them securely in place.

### 8 Add Baby's Breath

Cut small stems of baby's breath and push the stems into the foam to fill in around the roses.

### 7 Fill In Bouquet With Roses

Insert the roses in a circular arrangement, with two or three longer stems forming the cascade shape. The number of roses used in the cascade portion of the bouquet will determine its length. Continue filling in with more roses until the desired appearance is achieved.

## color Accent with Purple Statice
To add more color, use purple statice as an additional filler flower.

### 9 Store and Maintain Bouquet

This bouquet can be made up to three days in advance of the wedding. Keep it refrigerated or in a cold garage for storage. The roses will open up at room temperature. Rehydrate the floral foam bouquet holder once a day until the wedding by submerging the holder in water. Avoid getting the flowers wet. To avoid mildew, let the holder air dry before putting it back into the refrigerator.

florist **tip**

Roses should be inserted in bud form, but if a fuller rose is desired, leaving the bouquet at room temperature will cause the roses to open. When roses are open as desired, refrigerate the bouquet to keep the roses fresh.

### silk Cascade Bouquet with Fresh Roses
Here's another idea for a cascade bouquet, done with silk ivy, lilies, and baby's breath. To get the look of a fresh flower bouquet, add a few fresh red roses for color.

### silk Gardenia Cascade Bouquet
For a beautiful cascade bouquet done all in silk flowers, try this bouquet of gardenias, white roses, miniature pink roses, yarrow and leatherleaf.

# daisy & tulip

## nosegay

*This lovely round bouquet filled with gerbera daisies, roses, tulips, freesia, delphinium and Queen Anne's lace is perfect for a garden wedding. Finish it off with pearl-trimmed ribbon and a generous bow for a glorious spring bouquet.*

▸ **materials**

5 gerbera daisies

3–5 freesia

5 stems delphinium

4–8 tulips

2–3 stems Queen Anne's lace

3–12 color-tipped roses (optional)

leatherleaf and sprengeri fern

1 ½" (4cm) wide no. 9 ribbon

6" (15cm) wide tulle

floral wire and floral pick

straight-handled floral foam bouquet holder

tulle bouquet backing form

white floral tape

*1 Attach Foam Holder to Bouquet Back*

Soak the floral foam holder for fifteen minutes in water until it's completely saturated. Insert the foam holder into the tulle bouquet backing.

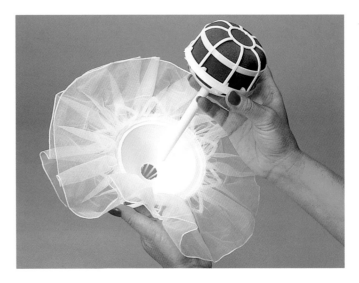

## 2 Secure Holder in Place

Pull the foam holder completely through the center of the backing form. When the holder is snug inside the backing, secure it with floral tape. Stretch the floral tape as it is being wrapped, molding the tape around the shape of the handle with your fingers.

## 3 Insert Leatherleaf

Cut the tips of the leatherleaf and strip the stems smooth. Insert the stems into the floral foam starting at the outside and forming a circle. Gradually make smaller circles as you get closer to the center of the holder.

## 4 Fill In With Sprengeri Fern

Cut tips of sprengeri and strip the stems. To remove the small thorns, wrap a lightweight towel around the stems and pull down tightly. Push stems of sprengeri into the floral foam to fill in. As you complete your bouquet, you can continue to add greenery to increase density. Leaf shine may be sprayed on the greenery at this stage if desired.

32

 florist **tip**

Visually, odd numbers of flowers look more attractive than even numbers.

## 5 Insert Gerbera Daisies

Cut five gerbera daisy stems. Determine stem length by holding the flower up to the bouquet and cutting to the desired length. Add approximately 1" (3cm) to allow for the part of stem that will be pushed into the holder (3" to 4" [8cm to 11cm] lengths were used in this example). Insert the first gerbera daisy into the center of the floral foam. Place four more around the center flower. If you change your mind about the placement of a flower, be sure to re-insert the stem into a new space in the foam so it won't fall out. If necessary, spray stems with stem adhesive to help secure them in place.

## 6 Add Delphinium

Insert small stems of delphinium into the floral foam to fill in around the gerbera daisies.

## 7 Add Tulips

Insert tulips randomly around the gerbera daisies.

## 8 Add Freesia

Insert freesia to fill in around the gerbera daisies.

## 9 Add Queen Anne's Lace

Cut individual florets of Queen Anne's lace from a branch, and insert the stems into the floral foam to fill in around the flowers.

## 10 Start the Bow

Keeping both the tulle and ribbon on their rolls, gather both materials and pinch them together between your fingers as you make the loops.

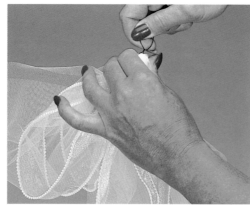

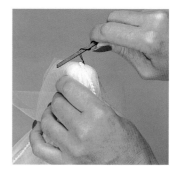

## 11 Make Loops

Increase the size of the loops as you go, starting with two 6" (16cm) loops, then two 8" (21cm) loops, and then two 10" (26cm) loops.

## 12 Secure Bow With Wire

Bend a length of floral wire around the center of the bow where you have been pinching it. Bring the ends of the wire together and with one hand, pull the center of the bow down into the wire firmly while holding the ends of the wire in the other hand. Twist the ends of the wire to secure tightly around the bow's center.

## 13 Finish Bow

Trim the ends of the ribbon and tulle to your desired length with an angle cut. Cut a floral pick to approximately 3" (8cm) using wire cutters. Secure the bow onto the floral pick by wrapping the wire ends around the stick.

## 14 Attach Bow to Bouquet

Insert the end of the floral pick into the floral foam at the base of the foam holder, directing the end of the pick at an angle toward the center of the bouquet.

## 15 Store and Maintain Bouquet

This bouquet can be made one day in advance of the wedding. Store it in the refrigerator to inhibit the growth of the tulips (cut tulips continue to grow in water). The bouquet can also be covered with a dark garbage bag with ventilation holes and stored in a cool, dry place such as a garage.

color Accent Variation

For a touch of color, add red-tipped white roses. Remember, when adding color accents to an all-white bouquet, odd numbers of flowers appear more attractive.

 silk Nosegay with Roses & Tulips

Using the same technique, you can make a beautiful silk nosegay bouquet that bursts with color. This bouquet uses silk cream roses, pink tulips, purple heather, hydrangea, sprengeri fern and leatherleaf. Combine three ribbons to create a coordinated bow.

# *white rose*

## nosegay

*Pure white bouquets are a symbol of traditional bridal elegance and style. Create this stunning nosegay of white roses, carnations and statice, then dress it up with a wired satin bow for a bouquet that is simply beautiful.*

⟩ **materials**

5 roses

3–4 stems miniature carnations

2–3 stems statice

2–3 stems waxflower

leatherleaf

3–7 sweetheart roses (optional)

1¹⁄₂" (4cm) wide wired ribbon
  (48"-60"[121cm-152cm])

floral wire

floral pick

floral foam bouquet holder

leaf shine

Flora Lock

### 1 Add Leatherleaf

Soak floral foam holder approximately fifteen minutes in water or until floral foam is completely saturated. Cut tips of leatherleaf and strip the stems at the base approximately 1" (3cm) from the bottom. Insert the leatherleaf in a circular manner around the base of the holder and continue to insert smaller tips towards the center of the holder. If desired, spray with leaf shine when greenery is completed.

## 4 *Add Statice*

Cut small stems of statice and strip them of loose foliage to make it easier to insert them into the foam. Insert statice randomly throughout the bouquet.

## 2 *Add Roses*

Cut rose stems to desired length and trim thorns. The length of the stems will vary depending upon the overall size of your bouquet, but generally stems should be 3" to 4" (8cm to 11cm) long. Begin inserting roses by placing one in the center of the bouquet and placing the others around the first rose. Use Flora Lock to secure the stems securely in the holder.

## 3 *Add Carnations*

Cut individual carnation stems to approximately 3" (8cm). Insert carnations randomly around the roses, keeping the outside shape of the bouquet round. To add interest to the bouquet, fill in with miniature carnation buds too. Spray Flora Lock on stems to hold them securely.

## 5 *Add Waxflower*

Cut pieces of waxflower, leaving approximately 2" or 3" (5cm or 8cm) stems. Clean stems of all foliage before inserting into the bouquet holder. Tuck stems of wax flower deep into the bouquet and cover the entire bouquet for an abundant, full look.

## 6 *Make Bow*

Make a standard floral bow with wired ribbon as described on page 21 of the Basic Techniques section. Cut the streamers on the bow to the desired length. Bend the ribbon streamers in and out with your fingers to create a ripple effect.

## 7 *Attach Bow to Floral Pick*

Cut a floral pick to 4" (11cm) with a pair of wire cutters. Wrap the ends of the floral wire at the center of the bow around the floral pick.

## 8 *Attach Ribbon to Bouquet*

Insert the end of the floral pick into the floral foam at the base of the holder, directing the end of the pick at an angle toward the center of the bouquet.

## 9 *Store and Mantain Bouquet*

You can make this bouquet up to three days in advance of the wedding. Store it in the refrigerator for two days and leave it out for twenty-four hours before the wedding to allow the roses to open. Rehydrate the floral foam holder daily by submering the holder in water without getting the flowers wet. Allow the holder to air dry before returning it to the refrigerator. The bouquet can also be stored in a cold, dry garage away from sunlight covered in a dark garbage bag with ventilation holes.

color Accent Variation

Here's a variation on our original bouquet with a touch of color added in the form of pink sweetheart roses

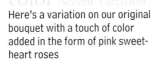

# biedermeier

## bouquet

*Create this vibrant Biedermeier bouquet of densely packed rings of flowers in an array of colors. Featuring lush red roses, pastel pink carnations, delicate alstroemeria, bright yellow button mums, lavender statice and a single coral rose, this bouquet is bound to draw all eyes to you.*

▸ **materials**

5–8 stems alstroemeria

20–36 roses

2–3 stems statice

8–10 stems miniature carnations

4–5 stems button mums

2–3 stems lemonleaf (salal)

straight-handled floral foam bouquet holder

leaf shine

Flora Lock

### 1 Insert Greenery

Soak the floral foam holder approximately fifteen minutes in water or until floral foam is completely saturated. Cut individual stems of lemonleaf and begin inserting in a circular manner only at the base of the foam holder. If desired, spray with leaf shine when greenery is completed.

## 2 Insert Center Flower

Insert a coral rose in the center of the foam holder. To ensure the stem stays in the holder, spray Flora Lock stem adhesive on the stem to hold it securely. Use stem adhesive on all the flower stems at each step to hold them securely and seal the moisture in the floral foam.

## 3 Add Statice

Cut short stems of statice approximately 2" to 3" (5cm to 8cm) long and begin inserting the stems into the floral foam around the center flower in a circular pattern. Place flowers close to one another to create a solid visual line.

## 4 Insert Button Mums

Cut mum stems approximately 2" to 3" (5cm to 8cm) in length and insert stems into the floral foam in a circular pattern around the statice. Again, place the flowers close to one another and use Flora Lock to secure the stems.

## 5 Add Alstroemeria

Cut stems approximately 2" to 3" (5cm to 8cm) in length and insert alstroemeria into the floral foam in a circular pattern around the mums. Keep the flowers close together and use Flora Lock to secure the stems.

## 6 Add Miniature Carnations

Cut carnation stems approximately 2" to 3" (5cm to 8cm) in length and insert them into the floral foam in a circular pattern around the alstroemeria. Place the flowers close together.

## 7 Add Final Circle of Roses

Cut stems of red roses approximately 2" to 3" (5cm to 8cm) in length and insert roses into the floral foam in a circular pattern around the carnations. Keep flowers close to one another to create a solid visual line. Spray Flora Lock on the stems to hold them securely.

## 8 Store and Maintain Bouquet

This bouquet can be made up to three days in advance of the wedding. Ideally, you should refrigerate the bouquet for two days and leave it out for a day to allow the roses to open to full bloom. You can also store the bouquet in a dark garbage bag with ventilation holes in a cool, dry space. Rehydrate the floral foam bouquet holder daily by submerging the holder in water without getting the flowers wet. Allow the holder to air dry before returning it to the refrigerator or storage bag to avoid mildew.

# *lily*
## crescent bouquet

*This simple yet elegant bouquet showcases an arrangement of white lilies and trailing dendrobium orchids. Symbolizing purity and sweetness, lilies are a classic choice for formal weddings. For a touch of dramatic color, add red gerbera daisies and strawberry bush.*

**▸ materials**

2–3 stems Stargazer lilies

4–6 stems dendrobium orchids

3–4 stems Italian ruscus

3–5 gerbera daisies (optional)

3–5 stems strawberry bush (optional)

large floral foam bouquet holder

leaf shine

Flora Lock

### 1 *Add Greenery to Holder*

Soak floral foam holder approximately fifteen minutes in water or until floral foam is completely saturated. Cut Italian ruscus into short, medium and long pieces and strip stems free of foliage approximately 1" (3cm) from the ends. Begin inserting long stems first, positioning them on the left and right sides, angling them downward to form the crescent shape. Add medium lengths to bottom front and one medium stem at the top, then continue adding smaller stems up toward the center of the holder. If desired, spray with leaf shine when greenery is completed.

### 2 Add Lilies

Cut two stems of lilies, leaving buds still attached, one for each side of the bouquet. Insert stems so the flowers flow downward into the crescent shape. Cut a single open lily and insert it into the center of the holder. Cut remaining unopened buds from stems and insert randomly in bouquet. Spray Flora Lock on the stems to hold them securely.

### 3 Add Orchids

Cut the orchid stems in fairly long, staggered lengths, and insert the two longest on the left and right to form the crescent shape . Fill in around the lilies with increasingly shorter lengths, working from the outside to the inside. One stem of orchids may be cut into more than one length, and these shorter pieces can be inserted into the bouquet around the lilies for filler. Use Flora Lock to secure the stems. The long, trailing orchids will form the dramatic design of the crescent shape and extend out beyond the lilies.

**variations**

### color Accent Variation

Want some color? Add dark red gerbera daisies and strawberry bush to create an even more dramatic appearance.

## 4 Store and Maintain Bouquet

You can make this bouquet a day in advance of the wedding. Store it in the refrigerator. If some of the lily buds begin to open, be sure to remove the stamens to avoid staining clothing.

### florist tip

Always remove the powdery stamens in the center of lilies. The powder will stain clothing and the stamens can draw bees. If you get some of the stamen powder on your clothes, do not try to rinse it out with water (this will only stain the fabric further). Instead use a pipe cleaner, chenille stem or lint brush to lift the powder out of the fabric.

### silk Crescent Bouquet with Stargazer Lilies

Try a crescent bouquet in silk flowers with Stargazer lilies, red and fuchsia roses, baby's breath, ivy and preserved plumosa.

# rose & lily

## hand-tied bouquet

This delicate hand-tied bouquet features white roses, lilies and delphinium for a feminine and fragrant arrangement. An elegant satin-edged ribbon completes this eternally romantic bridal bouquet.

**› materials**

3–5 stems lilies

3–7 roses

1–2 stems caspia

3–5 stems delphinium

5–7 stems coffee foliage

1 cable tie

satin ribbon

sheer ribbon

2–3 corsage pins

floral wire

### 1 Gather Lilies and Greenery

Before you begin assembling the bouquet, remove the foliage at the bottom of the stems of all the flowers you will be using. Begin the bouquet with one stem of coffee foliage and three lilies, arranging the coffee between the stems of lilies. Use one hand to arrange stems and the other to hold the flowers loosely in place.

## 4 Shape the Bouquet

Working with the flowers in your hand, begin to adjust the placement of the flowers to create the desired look.

## 2 Add Delphinium

Add delphinium stems by interspersing them between other loosely held stems in your hand so they are randomly spaced throughout the bouquet. Add a stem or two of foliage as needed.

## 3 Add Roses and Caspia

Add roses to the bouquet at varying heights. The outside roses should be brought in lower and the middle ones should be slightly taller to add dimension to the bouquet. Add caspia as a filler flower throughout the entire bouquet, making sure stems of caspia are placed on the outside perimeter of the bouquet to soften the appearance. Add foliage as needed.

## 5 Add Flowers and Foliage

To achieve a look of fullness in your bouquet, add flowers, foliage or filler flowers as needed. Work downward from the top of the bouquet to the bottom and continue shaping by placing stems at various heights.

## 6 Add Final Foliage

Add more foliage and arrange it at the base of the bouquet.

## 7 Tie Off Bouquet

Once you are sure of your arrangement, hold all of the stems firmly in one hand and wrap a cable tie around the stems to secure them. Insert one end of the cable tie through the loop and pull tight. Clip the excess end of the cable tie with wire cutters.

### 8 *Cut Stems*

Using clippers, trim all stems to desired length.

### 9 *Wrap Stems*

Wrap a satin ribbon around the stems of the flowers to conceal the cable tie and anchor it with two or three corsage pins. Insert the pins at a downward angle.

### 10 *Add Bow*

Using sheer ribbon, tie a standard bow following the directions on page 21 in the Basic Techniques section. Add another streamer onto the bow. Wrap the streamers around the stems, bring them back to the front and tie behind the finished bow with a square knot. Trim the streamers to your desired length with an angle cut.

### 11 *Store and Maintain Bouquet*

You can make this bouquet a day in advance of the wedding and keep it in a water-filled vase. Store it in a refrigerator or leave it out. When you remove it from the vase, be sure to dry the stems to keep the flowers from dripping down the aisle. The bouquet will be okay out of water for up to two hours.

### ❦ silk & dried flower
#### Hand-Tied Bouquet

Want a dried flower look for a fall wedding? Try this hand-tied bouquet using silk yarrow, silk larkspur, silk Queen Anne's lace and silk asters mixed with dried wheat and preserved plumosa. Gather the stems with raffia for a natural look.

Want to dress up a hand-tied bouquet? Try one of these ribbon techniques for creatively wrapping the stems of your bouquet for just that extra touch of sophistication and romance.

### FANCY RIBBON WRAP

**1** Place your ribbon under the stems at the bottom of the bouquet. Wrap the ribbon around the stems to the front of the bouquet and twist.

**2** Continue to wrap underneath the stems, bringing the ribbon forward and twisting all the way up the stems of the bouquet until you reach the base of the flowers.

**3** Tie off the ribbon at the top with a square knot.

**4** Finish the ends of the streamers with an angled cut. Fold the streamer ends in half lengthwise and cut upward at an angle. If you are using a wired ribbon as shown you can arrange the streamers as desired.

**1** Trim the sharp ends off three 2" (5cm) pearled corsage pins.

**2** Cut a 12" (31cm) length of ribbon or a length of ribbon that will allow you to wrap the bouquet stems four to five times around. Begin by holding one end of the ribbon securely against the stems and start wrapping the ribbon around the stems tightly.

**3** Continue wrapping the ribbon until the remaining end is ready to be anchored. Fold the end of the ribbon under for a finished edge and secure with the first corsage pin. Insert the corsage pin securely at a downward slant.

**4** Add the remaining corsage pins along the width of the ribbon until it is totally secure. More corsage pins may be needed if your ribbon is wider than 2" (5cm).

# *stephanotis*

## headband & bridal veil

*A beautiful bridal headpiece can complement any bouquet. This elegant headband veil is adorned with delicate silk stephanotis, silk baby's breath and silk ivy. A stylish accessory for any wedding gown, it also makes a wonderful keepsake for the bride.*

➤ **materials**

12 silk stephanotis blossoms

1 stem silk ivy

1 stem silk baby's breath

plastic headband

24" (60cm) wide tulle

white floral tape

floral adhesive

fabric glue (optional)

### 1 Prepare Silk Flowers

Cut small pieces of stephanotis, baby's breath and ivy.

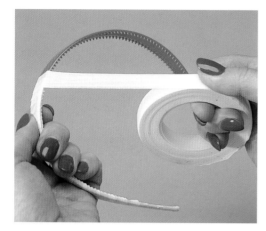

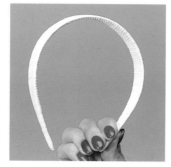

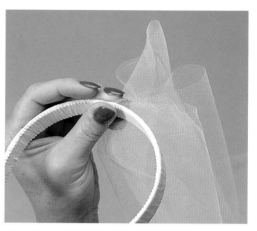

## 2 Wrap Headband

Beginning at one end of the headband, wrap white floral tape completely around the band to cover it. Cut the tape into shorter lengths to make it easier to wrap. Be sure to stretch the tape by pulling firmly with your fingers. The teeth of the headband should pierce through the tape.

## 3 Complete Taping

Wrap the headband twice if the original color of the headband is still showing through the floral tape. To finish wrapping, put a strip of floral tape on the tips of the band length-wise and mold it with your fingers for a smooth look.

## 4 Prepare Veil

Cut the tulle to 24" (60cm) wide. Use your own personal preference to decide on the length. Fold the veil three times on one end and place the folds flat on top of the headband.

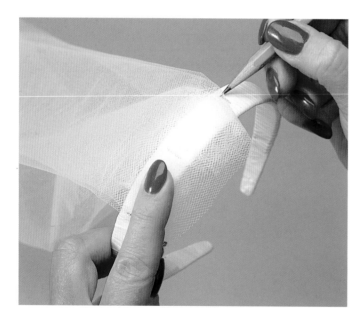

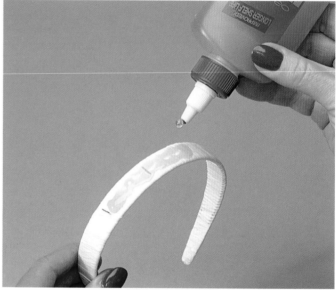

## 5 Center Veil on Headband

On the headband, mark with a pencil where the centered placement of the veil should be.

## 6 Add Glue to Headband

Put a moderate amount of floral adhesive on the head-band between your pencil marks. This is where the fold-ed veil will be secured. Let the adhesive become tacky for approximately one to two minutes.

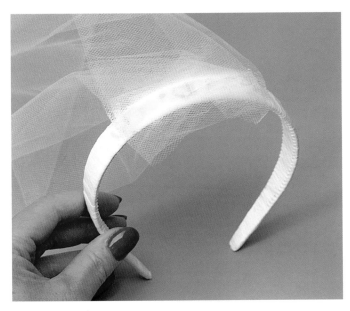

## 7 Secure Veil

Place the folded end of the veil on the floral adhesive in the center of the headband. Press firmly with your fingers to secure. Be sure to let the folded end of the veil extend over the headband approximately 1" (3cm). The veil can be trimmed to the headband later.

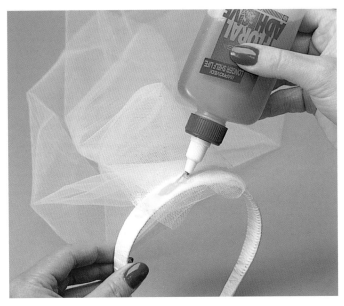

## 8 Add Glue to Veil

Put a moderate amount of floral adhesive on the top of the folded veil and smooth it with the end of the applicator or your finger. Dry on low with a hairdryer for ten minutes.

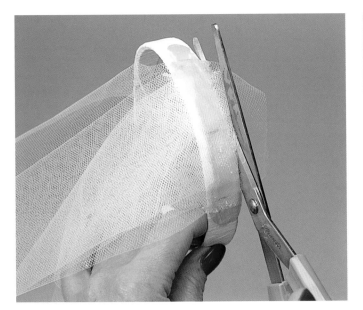

## 9 Trim Veil

Cut off the excess tulle in front of the headband with scissors.

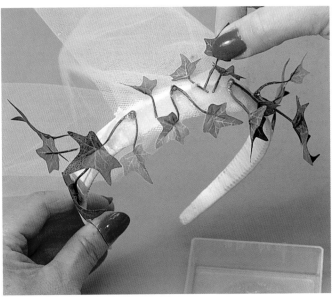

## 10 Add Silk Ivy

Put a small quantity of floral adhesive in a dish. Dip the ivy stems into the adhesive when it's tacky and place them on the headband, loosely covering the tulle on the band and around the edges. Be careful to only use a small amount of glue on the stems to keep the glue from running. Hold each stem briefly on the glue surface when securing. If the glue is tacky it will dry securely within thirty seconds.

## 11 Extend Ivy Over Headband

Extend the ivy over the front of the headband to create
softness around the face.

## 12 Add Silk Baby's Breath

Dip small pieces of baby's breath in the tacky adhesive
and place randomly on the headband around the ivy.

## 13 Add Silk Stephanotis

Dip individual stephanotis blossoms in the tacky adhesive and place them randomly among the ivy and baby's
breath. Continue adding flowers until the headband is as
full as desired.

## 14 Fill In Headband

To create an abundant look, add more baby's breath and
ivy where needed.

## 15 Add Details

If you want to embellish the veil, try using fabric glue to attach stephanotis blooms or sprigs of baby's breath randomly on the tulle. You can also use scissors to round the corners of the veil for a softer look.

## 1 Add Glue to Comb

Apply a line of floral adhesive to the entire length of the hair comb. Let the adhesive set for approximately one to two minutes (until it gets tacky) before adding flowers.

## 2 Add Baby's Breath

Put some floral adhesive in a small dish so it can begin to set up and get tacky. Cut small pieces of baby's breath and dip the stems in the adhesive. Layer the stems of baby's breath until the comb is covered.

# sweetheart rose

## hair comb

*Dress up an ordinary hair comb with fresh sweetheart roses. Great for an informal bride or bridesmaid, this hair comb is the perfect accent to any wedding hairstyle.*

**▸ materials**

3 sweetheart roses

1 stem baby's breath

hair comb

floral adhesive

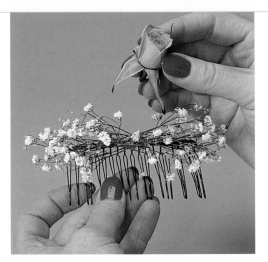

### 3 Add Sweetheart Roses

Cut individual sweetheart rose buds off at the base of the flower. Be sure to keep the outer green leaves around the buds. Dip three buds in the adhesive and attach them to the center of the hair comb in a triangle.

### 4 Store Finished Comb

The comb can be made up to three days in advance of the wedding. Store it in the refrigerator in a plastic bag with a few holes for ventilation to keep it from mildewing. After the wedding, just allow the flowers to dry naturally and save the comb as a lovely keepsake.

two

If the bride's bouquet is the crown jewel of the wedding, the bridesmaids' bouquets are the crown itself. The bride's flowers take precedence, but the bride's and bridal party flowers go hand in hand. The bride's bouquet sets the trend for the rest of the bridal party, so you want to have the bridal bouquet completely designed before selecting your attendants' bouquets. The bridesmaids' bouquets should look similar to the bride's in shape and color and coordinate with the ceremony and reception flowers. One way to do this is to have a signature flower that you can weave into all the arrangements to create continuity.

By this point you should know what your bridesmaids will be wearing, because their dresses will affect their bouquet selection. Be sure to create enough contrast between the attendants' dresses and their bouquets so that they do not completely blend into each other in the wedding photos. You don't want bridesmaids who are wearing crimson dresses to carry a bouquet filled with dark red roses; the roses will simply fade into the

dress. Also, consider the size and proportion of the bouquet in relation to the size of the person carrying it. Ideally you want to find a universal bouquet style that will complement each person.

Proportion is particularly important when choosing a bouquet or basket of flowers for your flower girl. Give her flowers that are easy to hold, light enough to carry and small enough not to trip her up. Flower halos or small pomanders are also charming accessories for young girls.

Finally, you might wish to have your maid or matron of honor carry a bouquet that's slightly different from the rest of the bridal party's bouquets. You can do this by adding a little more color to her bouquet, making it a bit larger or altering the style slightly. Whatever you choose, creating flowers for the bridal party provides a wonderful opportunity to give the gift of beautiful flowers to the important women in your life who are an integral part of your special day.

_flowers_
for the
_bridal
party_

63

# bridesmaid's
## bouquets

*Bridesmaids' bouquets should echo the color and shape of the larger bridal bouquet. Look at these examples to gather ideas on how to design and coordinate your bridal party bouquets.*

### Bride
Cascade Bouquet

### Bridesmaid
Cascade Bouquet

Made with the techniques on pages 26–29, this bridesmaid cascade bouquet is composed of Anna roses, waxflower, baby's breath and plumosa. To differentiate the bridesmaid bouquet from the bride's, it is smaller and uses fewer roses and more filler flowers. In addition, the bridesmaid cascade is shorter than the bride's with a subtle color change in the bouquet.

## Bridesmaid
### Nosegay

Yellow gerbera daisies, acacia, Queen Anne's lace and freesia comprise this colorful bridesmaid nosegay. Adding a burst of color and increasing the variety of flowers is a common way to design a bridesmaid bouquet and set it apart from the bridal bouquet. Follow the step-by-step techniques on pages 30–35 to create this relaxed, garden-style bridesmaid bouquet.

## Bride
### Nosegay

## Bride
Crescent Bouquet

## Bridesmaid Crescent Bouquet

Following the step-by-step techniques on pages 44–47, bring Stargazer lilies together with red roses, strawberry bush, dendrobium orchids and Italian ruscus to design this dramatic bridesmaid crescent bouquet. The bridesmaid bouquet is set apart from the bride's by its smaller crescent shape and bold color. The easiest way to design a bridesmaid crescent bouquet is by changing the focal flower. While typical bridal crescent bouquets feature gardenias, cymbidium orchids or large hybrid lilies, bridesmaid crescents feature gerbera daisies, fancy carnations, Stargazer and Asiatic lilies or Fuji mums.

# Bridesmaid Hand-Tied Bouquet

You can create this striking bridesmaid hand-tied bouquet featuring Asiatic lilies, roses, larkspur, asters, caspia, solidago and Italian ruscus by following the techniques on pages 48–51. This bridesmaid bouquet is set apart from the bride's with a burst of color and a greater variety of flowers. Another way to differentiate a bridesmaid hand-tied bouquet is to have shorter stems than the bridal bouquet. You can also completely ribbon-wrap the bridal bouquet stems and leave the stems showing in the bridesmaids' bouquets or ribbon-wrap the stems of the bridesmaids' bouquets in a different color.

# Bride
## Hand-Tied Bouquet

# sweetheart rose

## flower girl basket & halo

*Want to make your flower girl feel like a princess? Make this lovely halo wreath and coordinated flower basket designed with sweetheart roses and baby's breath. Fill the basket with handfuls of rose petals to be scattered before the bride.*

▶ **materials**

- 20–24 sweetheart roses
- 3–4 stems baby's breath
- rose petals or potpourri
- 6–8 stems plumosa
- basket
- sheer ribbon
- white floral tape
- floral wire
- chenille stems
- floral adhesive

**flower girl basket**

### 1 Add Greenery

Put a small amount of floral adhesive in a dish and let it set for one to two minutes or until the glue is tacky. Cut small sprigs of plumosa from the stem. Outline the top edge of the basket with adhesive. Place the pieces of plumosa around the basket edge. Continue to add greenery until you achieve the desired fullness.

## 4 Make Twist Ties

To make a twist tie, wrap a floral wire with white floral tape. To wrap the wire, start at one end, hold the end of the tape with one hand and smooth down with the other hand. Cover the entire wire evenly. Make two twist ties.

## 2 Add Baby's Breath

Cut small pieces of baby's breath from the stems. Dip individual stems into the adhesive and place them around the basket, randomly mixing them in with the plumosa.

## 3 Add Sweetheart Roses

Cut sweetheart rose buds from the stem. Put adhesive on the base of each rose and place them evenly around the basket, mixing them in with the baby's breath and plumosa. Depending on the size of your basket, you may want to use extra roses for fullness and color.

## 5 Attach Bows

Make two double loop bows following the techniques on page 21. Secure a bow to either side of the basket with the twist ties. Attach the bows at the base of each handle by wrapping the twist tie through the bow, around the handle and back to the front. Twist the wire under the bow so it will be secured and hidden. Fill the basket with rose petals or potpourri.

## 1 Size Halo

Twist two chenille stems together to form the halo. Measure the flower girl's head and form the halo to that measurement. Be careful not to make the halo too large so it won't slide down the flower girl's forehead.

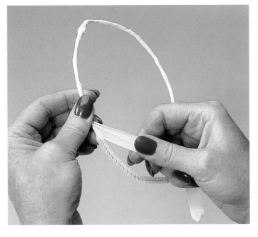

## 2 Wrap Chenille Stem Halo

Wrap short lengths (approximately 12" [31cm]), of white floral tape tightly around the halo. Remember to hold the halo with one hand and pull the tape with the other. Continue to wrap the tape around the halo until it's completely covered.

## 3 Add Baby's Breath

Cut small stems of baby's breath and dip each individual stem into the tacky floral adhesive you have put into a small dish. Press each stem onto the halo and hold for fifteen seconds or until it adheres securely. Continue adding flowers around the chenille halo form until you achieve the desired fullness. Be sure to use a very small amount of glue on each stem for best results.

## 4 Add Sweetheart Roses

Cut eight sweetheart rose buds from the stems, leaving only the flower head. Dip individual rose buds in the adhesive and glue them to the chenille halo form among the baby's breath. Place the roses evenly around the halo.

## 6 Store and Maintain

The rose halo and basket can be made up to three days in advance of the wedding if kept refrigerated. Attach the bows on the day of the wedding if the halo and basket will be stored in the refrigerator. You can make this project one day in advance of the wedding if it's kept in a cool, dry place away from sunlight, like a garage or basement. Remember, the larger the basket, the more flower petals you can fill it with so that your flower girl doesn't run out of petals before she reaches the altar. Also, be sure to check with your ceremony site to ask its policy on tossing flower petals on the floor.

## 5 Attach Bow

Make a twist tie following step 4 from the flower girl basket. Make a bow following the bow techniques on page 21, and tie it off with the twist tie. When making the bow it is nice to leave the streamers longer so they will trail down the back of the flower girl's head. Attach the bow to the halo using the twist tie. Twist the wire under the bow and cut the ends with wire cutters. Cut the streamers to the desired length.

# *flower girl*

## pomander

*Dozens of pastel roses accented with delicate waxflower create this charming pomander designed for a flower girl. An enchanting alternative bouquet for a little girl, the pomander hangs on a braided silk cord perfect for her little hands. After the wedding, allow the pomander flowers to dry as a keepsake for your special little bridesmaid.*

▸ **materials**

30–48 roses

waxflower

two floral igloo cages

floral adhesive

floral wire

silk cord

*1 Prepare Igloo Cages*

Soak the igloos in water for approximately fifteen minutes. Completely cover the bottom of both igloos with adhesive. Let them sit for one to two minutes until adhesive gets tacky.

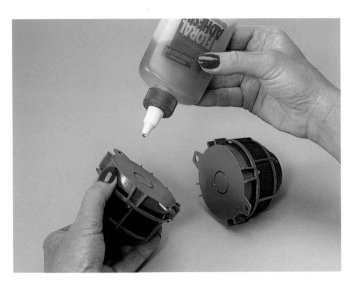

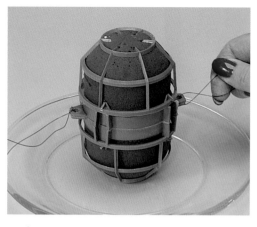

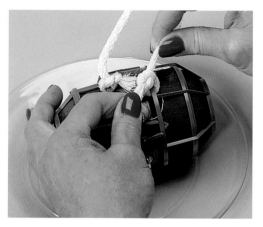

## 2 Join Igloo Cages

Press both igloos together to form a sphere, making sure the eyelets are lined up to match. Wipe off any excess glue with a damp towel.

## 3 Wire Igloo Cages

To secure the igloo cages together, put floral wire through the eyelets on both sides, pull tight and twist. Trim the ends of the wire with wire cutters and bend the twisted ends into the cage to hide them.

## 4 Add Handle

Lay the igloo on its side and pass the cording through the frame of the igloo just beside the eyelet. Tie it off with a square knot.

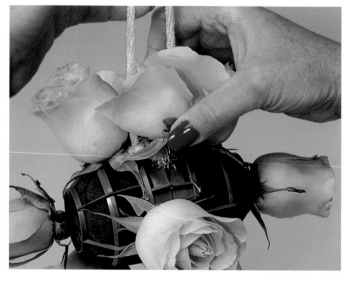

## 5 Insert Base Roses

Cut the stems of eight roses to approximately 2" (5cm) and remove the thorns. Place a rose in each end of the pomander. Next, place roses in a circular formation around the ball. Spray Flora Lock on all the rose stems to hold them securely in the floral foam.

## 6 Angle Roses

In order to cover the entire center frame of pomander, some roses should be inserted at an angle.

## 7 Fill In With Roses

Continue to insert roses around the pomander until it is completely covered. An alternate method of giving your pomander a nice dense look and saving money on the number of roses needed is to make use of greenery to fill in around the roses. The number of roses needed may also depend upon how open the blossoms are. Use Flora Lock to secure the stems.

## 8 Add Waxflower

Cut small sprigs of waxflower approximately 3" (8cm) long, stripping the foliage from the last inch of the stem. Insert waxflower randomly around the roses. Outer stems of waxflower may be trimmed with scissors if a more compact look is desired.

## 9 Store and Maintain

The rose pomander can be made three days in advance and hung in the refrigerator until four hours in advance of the wedding. Hang the pomander in a cool, dry place out of the sunlight for those few hours to allow the roses to open to full bloom. After the wedding, the pomander can be dried naturally. The flowers will shrink, however, when air-dried.

three

Although the bride's and bridesmaids' bouquets tend to get the most attention, the boutonnieres and corsages worn by the rest of the wedding party are an important floral accent as well. A beautifully designed boutonniere that goes perfectly with the groom's tux and the bride's bouquet can add a subtle but striking touch to the wedding.

Traditionally boutonnieres are worn by the groom, groomsmen, ushers, ring bearer, the fathers and grandfathers and—if you wish—the organist, soloist, readers and any other special male helpers. While the groom's boutonniere doesn't have to be larger than the others, it should stand out in some way. Consider using a different color or an altogether different flower than that featured on the other boutonnieres. One tip: Try to have a second boutonniere for the groom. Many grooms destroy their first boutonniere halfway into the reception (or earlier), thanks to all that hugging, kissing and dancing. A backup boutonniere will serve the groom well.

Traditionally you give corsages to the mothers, grandmothers and other women helping with or participating in the ceremony and reception. Corsages can be pinned on a dress or worn on the wrist. Ask the woman who will be wearing the corsage which type she would like (many mothers, for instance, might not want to put a pin through the costly material of a special dress and so prefer a wrist corsage or small bouquet).

When preparing flowers for your ring bearer, it's most important to keep proportion in mind; always go smaller rather than larger. The last thing you want is an unhappy little boy wearing a boutonniere so big it tickles his cheek and carrying a bulky pillow decorated with flowers that cover his face. You want your little guy to be comfortable, happy and handsome—just like the rest of the wedding party.

*flowers* for the *wedding party*

# corsage

Create cherished corsages for the mothers, grandmothers and other special women taking part in your ceremony. Champagne roses accented with waxflower and baby's breath make this corsage a special way to say thank you to the important women in your life.

♦ **materials**

5 roses

1–2 stems waxflower

1–2 stems baby's breath

1–2 stems coffee foliage

plumosa

sheer ribbon

green floral tape

floral wire

## 1 Make Foliage Cluster

Cut plumosa, coffee foliage and waxflower stems approximately 3" (8cm) long. Wrap floral wire around the stems approximately $1/2$" (2cm) from the bottom.

## 2 Fold Wire

Fold both ends of the wire down into stems.

## 3 Tape Stems

Hold the stems, wire and one end of the floral tape in one hand. Pull and stretch the floral tape downward as you rotate the stems between your fingers. Tear off the floral tape at the end and smooth it down along the stems.

## 4 Make Rose Cluster

Cut small sprigs of baby's breath and waxflower. Cut a rose with only $1/2$" (2cm) of stem.

## 5 Wire Flowers

Insert wire through the base of the rose while holding a sprig of baby's breath and waxflower around the rose. Fold the ends of the wire down into the stems.

## 6 Wrap Stems

Wrap the stems together with floral tape as before.

## 7 Make Additional Clusters

Make three additional foliage clusters for a total of four. Make four additional rose clusters for a total of five.

9 *Tape Clusters Together*

Using the green floral tape, tape both clusters together. Repeat steps 8 and 9 to make three clusters.

8 *Construct Top of Corsage*

Gather one foliage cluster and one rose cluster, placing the foliage cluster behind and above the rose cluster.

10 *Begin Arranging Corsage*

Arrange the three bundles together by staggering them in a triangle shape.

11 *Tape Top of Corsage*

Tape all three bundles together with floral tape.

12 *Add Rose Clusters*

Add the two remaining rose clusters, placing one below the other three roses. Place the last cluster in the middle. Tape all the stems together with floral tape.

13 *Add Foliage Clusters*

Add one foliage cluster behind the lower left-hand rose and another behind the lowest right-hand rose.

## 14 *Tape Stems*

Tape all the stems together with green floral tape.

## 15 *Add Bow*

Make a bow following the technique on page 21. Add the bow and the last foliage cluster to the base of the corsage. Wrap the stems with green floral tape.

## 16 *Trim Corsage Stem*

Cut the stem of the corsage to approximately 1½" (4cm) with wire cutters.

82

## 17 *Wrap Stems*

After the stems have been cut, wrap once more using green floral tape and smooth down to finish off.

## 18 *Store and Maintain*

The corsage can be made up to three days in advance. Store it in a refrigerator inside a plastic bag with holes for ventilation. Keep moisture out of the bag to prevent mildew. Before the wedding, pull off any damaged petals and leaves.

## ❧ silk *Rose Corsage*

Try this technique using silk roses and alstroemeria.

### WRIST CORSAGE

### RING PILLOW

This satin ring-bearer pillow can easily be embellished with a corsage to coordinate with the flower girl. To attach the corsage, use two corsage pins to pin the top and bottom of the corsage securely to the pillow.

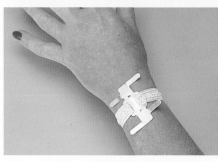

**1** Follow the step-by-step instructions on pages 79–82 to make a corsage. To attach it to your wrist you will need an elastic band wristlet.

**2** Attach the corsage to the wristlet by molding the metal tabs securely around the corsage stems.

**3** Wrap green floral tape around the wristlet ends.

# boutonniere

*A white rose boutonniere is a wonderful companion to any bridal bouquet. Usually composed of a single flower or small cluster of flowers, boutonnieres can be designed for all the honored men at your wedding—fathers, grandfathers, ushers, groomsmen and your groom.*

**▸ m a t e r i a l s**

rose and rose leaves

baby's breath

corsage pin

floral wire

green floral tape

### 1 Cut and Wire Flower

Cut the rose blossom at the base leaving approximately 1" (3cm) of stem. Cut the rose leaves off the stem and set them aside for later. Insert the wire through the base of the rose and pull the ends down around the stem.

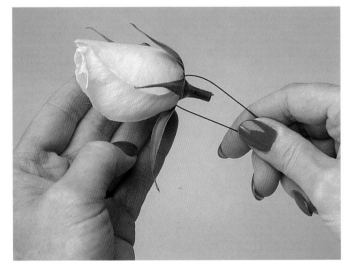

### 2 Tape Rose

Using green floral tape, wrap the rose stem and wire starting at the base of the rose. Hold the rose in one hand and twist slowly while pulling and stretching the floral tape with the other hand.

### 3 Wire Baby's Breath

Cut two stems of baby's breath with two small sprigs each. Bend a piece of floral wire over the stem of baby's breath and fold the ends down around stem. Wrap the stem and wire using green floral tape. Do this for both pieces of baby's breath. Only tape halfway down the wire.

### 4 Wire Leaves

Run the floral wire through the rose leaf on either side of the stem, then gently fold the ends of wire together around the base of the leaf to form a wire stem, being careful not to tear the leaf. Wrap the wire with green floral tape. Only tape halfway down the stem. Repeat this step for a second leaf. Spray the leaves with leaf shine.

### 5 Arrange Rose and Leaf

Place one leaf behind the rose.

### 6 Arrange Baby's Breath

Place a stem of baby's breath behind the rose.

### 7 Wrap Stems

Using green floral tape, wrap all stems securely.

## 8 Complete Arrangement

Add a rose leaf behind and slightly higher than the first rose leaf. Place the second sprig of baby's breath in front of and below the rose.

## 9 Wrap Stems

Bring all the stems together and wrap them with green floral tape. Trim the wire ends with wire cutters to a length of approximately 3" or 4" (8cm or 10cm).

## 10 Wrap Stem End

Wrap the end of the stem lengthwise with floral tape to cover the wire ends. Wrap the tape up and down the stem, molding the tape as you go.

## 11 Spiral the Stem

Wrap the wire stem around a pencil to form a spiral.

## 12 Store and Maintain

Boutonnieres can be made three days in advance of the wedding. Store them in the refrigerator in plastic bags with holes for ventilation. Boutonnieres for the grooms-men should complement the bridesmaid's bouquets.

four

Every wedding ceremony should look unique and have its own character. The special characteristics of your ceremony site should drive your floral decisions. Some churches, for instance, are so lavishly decorated themselves they only need a few strategically placed arrangements. If it's an outdoor garden wedding, work with the flowers that are all around you. Keep the focal points for your ceremony flowers near the bride and groom. But remember to leave enough open space so the guests can visually breathe and their eyes can easily focus on the bride and groom.

Ideally, you want to carry over your floral theme from the ceremony to the reception. It's common to introduce more flowers and color into the reception, since that's where you'll spend most of your time. To continue the floral theme at the reception, you can carry over the same flower that was dominant during the ceremony or a similar one. One way to do this is to have the bridesmaids carry one noticeable flower that

will also be featured as part of the reception table arrangements. When designing your reception table centerpieces, make sure your table flowers are light and airy enough so that conversation can easily go on around, over or through them. The important thing is not to restrict yourself to any set trend when doing your reception flowers—have fun and experiment. Just remember your wedding and reception flowers should be tied together as a package to create an overall ambiance.

One place you can create special flower decorations is on the cake table. Floral cake tops are a great way to add color to your wedding cake, and garlands are a lovely floral accent to drape around the cake table. However, be careful not to overdo it. Cake table flowers should only be a complement to an already gorgeous wedding cake and reception.

89

*flowers*
for the
*ceremony*
& *reception*

# unity candle

## arrangement

*Lighting the unity candle is a symbolic part of many wedding ceremonies. Celebrate your union with this lush unity candle arrangement of alstroemeria, acacia, freesia and baby's breath.*

### ▸materials

4–5 stems alstroemeria

5–8 stems freesia

acacia

plumosa

baby's breath

lemonleaf (salal)

unity or pillar candle 10" to 12" (25cm to 30cm)

two 15" (38cm) taper candles

floral adhesive

two floral foam bricks

4" x 18" (11cm x 93cm) green plastic tray

$^1/_4$" (5mm) wide floral foam tape

### 1 Form Base

Soak the floral foam in water until it is completely saturated. Put the floral foam in the tray and cut each brick to fit leaving an open space in the middle to accomodate the width of the unity candle.

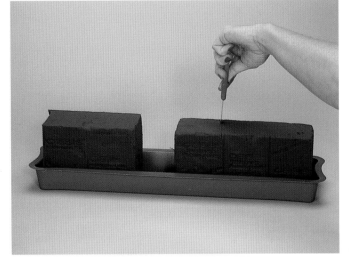

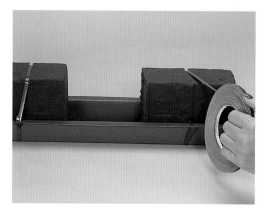

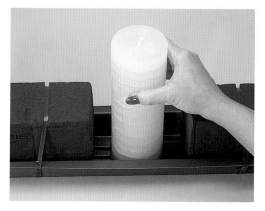

### 2 Tape Floral Foam

Tape the bricks in the tray using the floral foam tape. Wrap the tape all the way around the tray and the floral foam. Make sure the tape is slightly off center to allow placement of the taper candles.

### 3 Add Floral Adhesive

Place floral adhesive on the bottom of the tray where the unity candle will be placed.

### 4 Place Unity Candle

Cover the bottom of the unity candle with adhesive. Wait a minute or two until the glue is tacky and then place the candle firmly down into the tray, making sure to center it.

### 5 Place Taper Candles

Push the taper candles into the floral foam firmly, making sure each candle goes in straight. If the candle is not straight or is loose, place floral adhesive on the candle base and inside the hole and reinsert the candle after the glue becomes tacky. This will hold the candles firmly in place.

### 6 Add Greenery

Trim the lemonleaf stems into sprigs and begin to insert them around the lower base of the floral foam. Make sure the leaves cover the tray, all of the floral foam and the area around the base of the unity candle.

### 7 Fill In With Leaves

Fill in with small pieces where needed to cover the base. Spray all the greenery with leaf shine.

### 8 Add Baby's Breath

Cut small sprigs of baby's breath and insert them randomly between the lemonleaf. Some leaves may have to be lifted to insert the baby's breath stems into the floral foam.

## 9 Add Plumosa

Cut small sprigs of plumosa and insert them randomly throughout the arrangement.

## 10 Add Alstroemeria Around Candles

Cut two stems of white alstroemeria so that three or four flowers remain on the stem. Insert one stem at the base of each taper candle.

## 11 Add Alstroemeria to Base

Cut individual blossoms of yellow alstroemeria from the stems and insert as desired across the front of the arrangement.

## 12 Add Freesia

Cut freesia stems approximately 4" (11cm) in length and add as desired around the base.

## 14 Store and Maintain

This arrangement can be made up to two days in advance of the wedding. Store it in a cool, dark place and water regularly. Make sure the candles have good wicks for ease in lighting. Loosen the taper candles from the foam before the ceremony to make them easy to pick up.

## 13 Add Acacia

Cut sprigs of acacia with approximately 4" to 6" (11cm to 16cm) stems and insert randomly as desired.

# silk ivy

## pew decoration

*Line your wedding aisle with these dramatic silk pew decorations. Trailing ivy is the backdrop for brilliant red roses and spectacular lilies. Just add a sheer ribbon bow for the final touch.*

### ▸ materials

3–7 stems silk lilies

3–9 silk roses, open

4–6 stems silk baby's breath

corkscrew willow branches

silk ivy bushes (one large bush with long trailers and one small bush)

open floral cage

dry sahara foam (one brick)

2½" (6cm) wide sheer ribbon

¼" (5cm) wide floral foam tape

floral wire

green chenille stems

floral pick

green floral tape

### 1 Prepare Floral Cage

Insert the dry foam brick into the cage and tape it into place with floral foam tape.

## 2 *Insert Ivy*

Insert the large ivy bush into the side of the cage approximately two-thirds of the way up. Make sure the stem is pushed firmly in at an angle.

## 3 *Arrange Ivy*

Open the bush with your hands and unfold the individual stems in an attractive manner around the cage, making sure the longest trails of ivy are at the bottom.

## 4 *Cover the Cage*

Cut sprigs of ivy from the second ivy bush and insert them into the sides of the cage to completely hide the cage. Add more sprigs as needed to cover the entire cage. Both the sides and front of the cage should be entirely covered with ivy, leaving the back uncovered so it can rest flat against the pew.

## 5 *Attach Hanger*

Loop a chenille stem through the center bars of the back of the cage just below the top and twist them together. Although this hanger may not be necessary during the ceremony (depending upon various facility accommodations), the hanger will allow the arrangement to also be displayed on a wall, stairway or candelabra.

## 6 *Add Baby's Breath*

Cut sprigs of baby's breath and place them randomly throughout the ivy.

## 7 *Add Bow*

Make a standard bow with extra streamers. Wire the center with floral wire, and attach to a floral pick by wrapping with floral tape. Insert the completed bow by pushing the floral pick into the dry foam slightly above the center of the cage in the front. Fluff and arrange the loops of the bow. Allow the ivy to intertwine with the loops.

### 8 Add Lilies

Cut individual lily blossoms from the stems with varying lengths of stem remaining. Arrange the lilies randomly in the bouquet using shorter flowers in the middle and longer stems in the top, bottom and sides.

### 9 Add Roses

Cut rose stems to varying lengths of 6" to 10" (16cm to 26cm) and place as desired. The color of the roses should be the accent color used throughout the wedding and may coordinate with the bridesmaids' dresses.

### candelabra Variation

Use the same pew decoration to adorn a candelabra. Candelabras can be rented or may be available at a church. Just hang the pew decoration on the candelabra with chenille stems for a striking display.

### 10 Add Willow Branches

Cut willow branches as desired and add randomly to the arrangement.

### 11 Attach Arrangement

Contact the ceremony site for placement and attachment requirements.

# *flower*

## garland

*Create a dramatic doorway with a garland bursting with spring flowers. Luscious greenery is entwined with alstroemeria, waxflower, strawberry bush, baby's breath and caspia for a decorative garland perfect for draping anywhere—from doors, arches and windows to tables, candelabras and chairs.*

▸ **materials**

alstroemeria

waxflower

caspia

strawberry bush

coffee foliage

plumosa

baby's breath

paddle wire

petite water tubes

### 1 Remove Thorns

If the stems of plumosa are thorny, use a hand towel to safely strip the thorns off.

## 2 *Begin Garland*

Start by crisscrossing two stems of plumosa and wrapping paddle wire around the center to secure the stems together. This will create one end of the garland.

## 3 *Continue Adding Stems*

Begin to form the garland by adding more stems of plumosa.

## 4 *Layer Stems*

Layer each stem or stems (depending on desired fullness) one after the other.

## 5 *Wrap Stems With Wire*

To secure the stems of plumosa, hold the garland with one hand and wrap the paddle wire around it with the other. The paddle wire should be wrapped over some branches, but others can be loose and free.

## 6 *Cut Stems*

Any excess stem may be cut with clippers as you form the garland.

## 7 *Finish Plumosa*

Continue adding plumosa until the desired length is reached. Finish off the end of the garland by adding the last plumosa stem in a crisscross fashion. Make a slip knot with the paddle wire to secure it at the end of the garland.

100

florist **tip**

Longer stems are easier to wrap into the garland and add fullness.

## 8 *Add Baby's Breath*

Cut branches of baby's breath and space them along the garland. Wrap the stems into the garland with paddle wire.

## 9 *Add Coffee Foliage*

Cut stems of coffee foliage and lay them underneath the entire length of the garland. Wrap paddle wire from one end to the other to secure the stems to the garland.

florist **tip**

Wrap the paddle wire continually from one end of the garland to the other as more materials are added. You will not cut the wire until the very end.

## 10 *Add Caspia*

Cut pieces of caspia and randomly place them along the garland. Secure them by wrapping with paddle wire from one end to the other.

## 11 *Add Strawberry Bush*

Cut branches of strawberry bush and place along the garland. Wrap with paddle wire to secure.

## 12 *Add Waxflower*

Add stems of waxflower to the garland and wrap with paddle wire.

## 13 *Add Alstroemeria*

Cut stems of alstroemeria approximately 8" (21cm) long and insert into water-filled tubes. Place the flowers in various directions along the garland. Wrap paddle wire around the water tubes to secure them in the garland.

## 14 *Secure Flowers*

Wrap the paddle wire once more around the completed garland to secure everything. Wrap wire under individual flowers and foliage as needed. Cut the wire and bend the ends into the center of the garland.

## 15 *Store and Maintain*

The garland can be made up to forty-eight hours in advance of the wedding. To prevent wilting, lightly mist the garland, then coil it inside a dark plastic bag with a few air holes. Store it in a cool, dark place.

# candle

## centerpiece

*Illuminate your reception with beautiful candle centerpieces. Pefect for lining the bridal table or as guest table centerpieces, this arrangement composed of freesia, alstroemeria, waxflower, baby's breath and acacia is bound to catch everyone's attention.*

**▸ materials**

3 freesia

3–5 alstroemeria

1–2 stems waxflower

1–2 stems baby's breath

2–3 stems acacia

plumosa

lemonleaf (salal)

pillar candles (various heights)

floral igloo cage

floral adhesive

cardboard

leaf shine

### 1 Trace Candle

Trace around the base of the candle onto the cardboard.

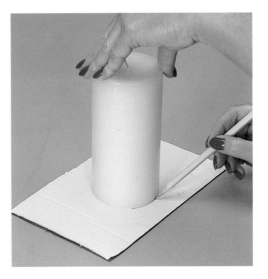

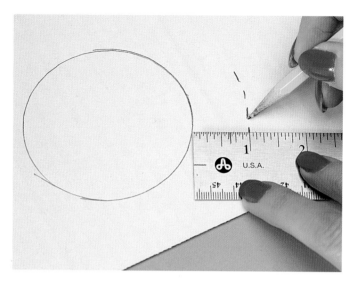

## 2 *Extend Circle*

Remove the candle from the cardboard and extend the circle by 1" (3cm) all around. Cut out the larger cardboard circle.

## 3 *Glue Lemonleaf*

Put floral adhesive on the outside inch of the cardboard circle and let it sit a minute or two until the glue gets tacky. Cut lemonleaf from their stems and place a small amount of floral adhesive on the back of each leaf toward the base of the leaf. Let the glue sit and get tacky. Attach the leaves to the outer edge of the cardboard circle, overlapping the leaf edges for complete coverage.

## 4 *Add Second Layer of Lemonleaf*

Add a second layer of lemonleaf in a slightly smaller circle than before, using the same technique as in the previous step. The second layer should begin inside the candle outline so that the cardboard will be completely covered by the candle. If desired, spray leaves with leaf shine.

## 5 *Place Candle*

Place the candle on the leaf ring, making sure there is no cardboard showing. It is not necessary to glue the candle to the ring.

## 6 Add Greenery to Floral Cage

Soak the floral foam igloo cage in water for approximately fifteen minutes or until it's saturated. Cut lemonleaf with short stems and insert them randomly around the base of the cage so that the layer of leaves lies flat around the cage. Spray with leaf shine if desired.

## 7 Add Plumosa

Cut short sprigs of plumosa and insert them randomly to cover the cage.

## 8 Add Freesia

Cut stems of freesia to varying heights and insert them into the top of the cage.

## 9 Add Baby's Breath

Cut sprigs of baby's breath and insert them randomly throughout the floral foam.

### 10 Add Acacia

Cut short sprigs of acacia and insert them randomly throughout the arrangement.

### 11 Add Alstroemeria

Cut short stems of alstroemeria and insert them randomly as desired.

### 12 Add Waxflower

Cut varying heights of waxflower and insert them throughout the arrangement as desired. Put the tallest sprig in the center.

### 13 Fill In Arrangement

Inspect the arrangement and fill in where necessary with additional flowers and greenery.

## 14  Store and Maintain

The floral cage arrangement can be made up to forty-eight hours in advance of the wedding. The lemonleaf candle rings can be made twenty-four hours in advance of the wedding. Both can be stored in the refrigerator or in a dark, cool place.

# *garden*

## table wreath

*Brighten up your reception tables with garden table wreaths bursting with color. This lush arrangement features alstroemeria, miniature carnations and daisy mums. Perfect for an outdoor wedding, a floating flower or candle in the center of this wreath adds the finishing touch.*

**▸ materials**

4–6 stems miniature carnations

2–3 stems alstroemeria

6 daisy mums

1 gerbera daisy

baby's breath

sprengeri fern

brandy snifter

foam plate

floral foam ring

### 1 Create Floating Flower

Cut a gerbera daisy and leave the stem about 2" (5cm) long. The stem will help balance the flower when it is floated on the water. Cut a circle out of the foam plate slightly smaller than the diameter of the flower. Poke a hole in the center of the foam disk using a pencil point. Insert the gerbera daisy in the hole.

## 2 Add Sprengeri

Cut a sprig of sprengeri and insert it through the hole next to the flower. Insert additional sprigs of sprengeri crisscrossing them behind and around the flower for balance.

## 3 Add Baby's Breath

Cut small sprigs of baby's breath and insert them through the hole, crisscrossing around the flower and greens.

## 4 Float Flower

Fill the brandy snifter a third of the way full with water and float the flower.

## 5 Add Greenery to Wreath

Soak the floral foam ring in water for approximately fifteen minutes or until saturated. Cut small sprigs of sprengeri and strip the stems so approximately ½" (2cm) is clean of leaves. Sprengeri has small thorns so use a cloth or paper towel to strip the stems. Insert sprengeri sprigs evenly around the top and sides of the wreath. Spray greens with leaf shine if desired.

## 6 Add Baby's Breath

Cut small sprigs of baby's breath and insert randomly throughout the wreath.

## 7 Add Daisy Mums

Cut daisy mums to desired length and insert randomly throughout the wreath.

## 8 *Add Alstroemeria*

Cut stems of alstroemeria and insert randomly through-out the wreath.

## 9 *Add Miniature Carnations*

Cut stems of miniature carnations and insert randomly throughout the wreath.

## 10 *Store and Maintain*

The table wreath can be made up to forty-eight hours in advance of the wedding. Keep it hydrated by placing it in a low pan with 1" (3cm) of water. Store it in the re-frigerator or a dark, cool place. Once the wreath is completed, leave it plain or weave sheer rib-bon around it as a variation. Spritz lightly with water before placing the wreath on a reception table.

# *ivy plant*

## centerpiece

*Dazzle your reception guests with this exquisite ivy plant centerpiece surrounded by soft candlelight. Simply add gerbera daisies, roses, strawberry bush and baby's breath to a potted ivy plant to create a romantic centerpiece in minutes.*

### ▸ materials

ivy plant with long trailers in a 6" or 8" (16cm or 21cm) pot

3–6 gerbera daisies

3–6 roses

2–3 stems strawberry bush

baby's breath

large water tubes

sphagnum moss

floral adhesive

### 1 Cover Plant Pot With Moss

Apply floral adhesive to the entire pot and let it stand for a minute or two until the glue is tacky. Take a section of sphagnum moss, moisten it by dipping it in a dish of water, then squeeze out the excess water with your hands. Apply floral adhesive to the back of the moss, and apply the moss around the pot. Continue applying sections of moss until the entire pot is completely covered.

### 2 *Add Baby's Breath*

Place the covered ivy pot on a table and spread out the ivy trailers as desired. Cut substantial sprigs of baby's breath and place them in water-filled tubes. Insert the tubes of baby's breath into the soil around the ivy plant at various angles as shown. The length of the stems and amount of baby's breath used should be proportional to the size of the table that the centerpiece is to be placed upon.

### 3 *Add Strawberry Bush*

Cut various lengths of strawberry bush stems and insert them at various angles into the soil around the ivy plant.

**florist tip**

Some flowering foliages do not need to be placed in water-filled tubes because the dampness in the soil will provide enough moisture for them. These include strawberry bush, statice, waxflower, caspia and yarrow.

114

### 4 *Add Gerbera Daisies*

Cut gerbera daisy stems at varying lengths and place in water tubes. To create height in your arrangement, place the tallest gerbera daisy in the center top of the arrangement, then place the remaining blooms randomly throughout the arrangement as desired.

## 5 Add Roses

Cut rose stems at varying heights and place in water tubes. Place roses randomly throughout the arrangement at various levels.

## 6 Complete Arrangement

This is a one-sided arrangement. If the arrangement is to be viewed from both sides, be sure to fill in with flowers on all sides. The arrangement can be made up to twenty-four hours in advance of the wedding.

# *gerbera daisy*

## topiary
*Gerbera daisies burst with color in this delightful topiary centerpiece perfect for a garden reception. Cover the terra-cotta pot with lemonleaf and embellish the topiary with colorful streamers to top off this festive arrangement.*

▸ **materials**

8 gerbera daisies

2–4 stems waxflower

2–3 stems acacia

2–3 stems lemonleaf (salal)

sphagnum moss

5" (13cm) terra-cotta clay pot

floral foam brick

dark green floral tape

floral wire

two types of $1^7/_8$" (4cm) wide sheer ribbon

floral adhesive

duct tape

light green chenille stems

### 1 *Cover Base of Pot*

Cover the hole in the bottom of the pot with a 2" (5cm) square of duct tape. Cut individual lemonleaf leaves from the stem. Place a thin covering of floral adhesive on the entire back of each leaf and let stand for a minute or two until glue is tacky. Cover the entire clay pot with floral adhesive and let it stand until the glue is tacky. Place the leaves around the base of the clay pot as shown.

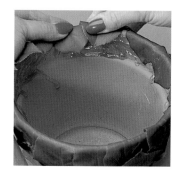

## 2 Layer Leaves

Place lemonleaf around the sides of the clay pot near the bottom and press the tips of the bottom leaves over them. Press only the bottoms of the leaves at this time because you will be putting additional leaves under the tips in the next step.

## 3 Add Leaves to Top of Pot

Cover the top of the pot with floral adhesive and let it sit until tacky. Continue to cover with leaves, inserting them under the tips of the previous layer and pressing them into place.

## 4 Cover Top Edge of Pot

Cover the inside of the top edge of the clay pot with adhesive and when it becomes tacky, roll the leaf tips over to the inside of the pot and press down.

## 5 Insert Floral Foam

Soak the floral foam in water for approximately fifteen minutes or until saturated. Push the brick of foam firmly down into the pot and cut it even with the top of the pot.

## 6 Cover Foam With Moss

Moisten the sphagnum moss by dipping it in water and squeezing the excess moisture out with your hands. Mold the moss over the floral foam and into the pot. (It is not necessary to glue the moss down.)

## 7 Prepare Gerbera Daisies

Gerbera daisies will flop over if the stems are not supported properly. To do this, insert a length of floral wire through the base of the flower.

## 8 Secure Wire

Push the wire up through the center of the flower and form a loop in the wire. Pull the wire loop down into flower so it is hidden.

## 9 Wrap Stem With Wire

Wrap the wire around the stem to straighten it and add stability.

## 10 Tape Stem

Wrap the stem with green floral tape, pulling and stretching the tape as you twist the stem.

## 11 Strengthen Stem

For added stability, a chenille stem can be fed up through the center of the gerbera daisy stem. Push the chenille stem up into the stem until it stops, then trim off the excess.

### 13 Add Gerbera Daisies

Insert three gerbera daisies at varying heights. Add additional gerbera daisies and waxflower stems as a filler flower until you reach the desired fullness.

### 12 Insert Acacia

Insert a tall, full stem of acacia into the center of the floral foam. If one stem is not full enough, add another for more fullness.

### 14 Add Ribbons

Cut each color of ribbon to approximately 36" (93cm) in length and tie in a square knot at the base of flowers to secure stems and form the topiary. The ribbon can be left as a square knot or a shoestring bow may be added. Trim ribbon streamers to desired length.

### 15 *Add Gerbera Daisy to Base*

Insert one short-stemmed gerbera daisy at an angle into the floral foam just above the moss.

### 16 *Add Acacia to Base*

Cut two short sprigs of acacia and insert them on either side of the gerbera daisy.

### 17 *Add Waxflower to Base*

Cut two short sprigs of waxflower and insert them close to the gerbera daisy.

### 18 *Store and Maintain*

The topiary can be made up to twenty-four hours in advance of the wedding. Store it in a cool, dark place and water it to keep it moist.

# *wedding*

## cake top

*Adorn your cake with fresh flowers by creating this beautiful cake top with roses, waxflower, acacia, strawberry bush and baby's breath. Add sprigs of waxflower around the cake tiers and circle the base with flowers for a stunning wedding cake presentation.*

**▶ materials**

3 roses

1 stem waxflower

1 stem acacia

1 stem strawberry bush

1 stem baby's breath

1–2 stems plumosa

1–2 stems coffee foliage

large floral foam igloo

### 1 *Add Greenery to Floral Foam*

Soak the floral foam igloo in water for approximately fifteen minutes or until saturated. Cut short sprigs of coffee foliage and insert to cover the base of cage. The diameter of the cage with greenery should be slightly larger than the diameter of the cake top.

## 2 Layer Coffee Foliage

Continue to insert coffee sprigs, layering up toward the center. Insert sprigs in the top and add more sprigs if necessary to create an even dome shape.

## 3 Add Plumosa

Cut sprigs of plumosa and insert them randomly throughout the floral cage.

## 4 Add Roses

Cut three roses with 3" (8cm) stems and insert around base.

## 5 Add Strawberry Bush

Cut sprigs of strawberry bush to various lengths and insert into the floral foam, placing the tallest one on top.

## 6 Add Baby's Breath

Cut various lengths of baby's breath and insert randomly throughout the arrangement.

## 7 Add Waxflower

Cut various lengths of waxflower and fill in randomly as desired.

## 8 Add Acacia

Cut various lengths of acacia and add as desired.

## 9 Store and Maintain

The cake top can be made up to forty-eight hours in advance of the wedding. Put it in a low pan with 1" (3cm) of water to keep it hydrated. Store it in the refrigerator or in a cool, dark place. If you want to embellish the cake further, cut small clusters of waxflower, acacia or baby's breath and place them around each cake tier. Be careful not to dig into the icing. You can also ask the bakery that makes your cake to place the flowers on the cake for you.

**Botanique Preservation Equipment, Inc.**
16601 N 25th Ave., Ste. 101
Phoenix, AZ 85023
(602) 993-3364
Fax: (602) 993-3285
www.botaniquefrzdry.com
—information on flower preservation and freeze drying

**Design Master Color Tool Inc.**
P.O. Box 601
Boulder, CO 80306
(303) 443-5214
Fax: (303) 443-5217
www.dmcolor.com
—floral scents, floral color sprays, paints and tints

**John Henry Company**
5800 Grand River Ave.
P.O. Box 17099
Lansing, Michigan 48901-7099
(800) 748-0517
Fax: (800) 968-5646
www.jhc.com
—leaf shine, floral preservatives and other floral supplies

**Knud Nielsen Company, Inc.**
P.O. Box 746
Evergreen, AL 36401
—dried flowers and foliage

**C.M. Offray & Son, Inc.**
360 Route 24
Chester, NJ 07930
(800) 551-LION
www.offray.com
—wide range of decorative ribbons

**Mariemont Florist, Inc.**
7257 Wooster Pike
Cincinnati, OH 45227
(800) 437-3567
Fax: (513) 271-7484
www.mariemontflorist.com
—contact author, general information and assistance

**Oasis Floral Products**
P.O. Box 118
Kent, OH 44240
(800) 321-8286
Fax: (800) 447-0813
—bouquet holders and other floral foam products

**Pokon Chrysal**
3063 N.W. 107th Ave.
Miami, FL 33172
(800) 247-9725
Fax: (305) 477-0112
www.pokonchyrsalusa.com
—floral preservative and leaf shine products

**Society of American Florists**
1601 Duke St.
Alexandria, VA 22314
(800) 336-4743
www.safnow.org
—general information about the floral industry

**VABAN Ribbon**
165 Eighth St.
San Francisco, CA 94103
(800) 448-9988
Fax: (415) 255-2329
—decorative ribbons

**W.J. Cowee, Inc.**
28 Taylor Ave.
P.O. Box 248
Berlin, NY 12022
(800) 658-2233
Fax: (518) 658-2244
www.cowee.com
—floral picks and general floral supplies

**Florist Directory**
www.eflorist.com
—web directory to assist in finding a florist in your area

# index

128